Avian Deities Birds In Mythology Across Cultures

By
Ehsan Sheroy

INDEX

Page Nos

INTRODUCTION

Birds have long caught the human creative mind with their ethereal beauty, taking off through skies and winding around complicated designs in the air. Past their actual presence, these animals have taken on significant representative importance in the legends of assorted societies since forever ago. From the grand bird of prey headed god Horus in old Egypt to the respected Garuda of Hindu folklore, the avian domain has filled in as a rich embroidery for the investigation of the heavenly, the otherworldly, and the emblematic.

This book, "Wings of Eternality: Avian Gods and Birds in Folklore Across Societies," sets out on an excursion to unwind the many-sided snare of convictions, stories, and social understandings encompassing avian divinities and birds in legends around the world. As we dig into the stories woven by various civic establishments, we find a consistent idea interfacing humankind's shared mindset across existence — the persevering through interest with birds as couriers of the heavenly, images of opportunity, and conductors among natural and divine domains.

1. Characterizing Avian Divinities and their Importance

The expression "avian gods" alludes to divine substances that manifest as birds or have avian characteristics. Birds, in different legendary settings, rise above their natural presence, representing the extension between the human and the heavenly. Their capacity to cross the sky makes them strong delegates, couriers conveying messages from the divine beings to mankind as well as the other way around. As we leave on this investigation, it becomes clear that the emblematic load of avian divinities stretches out past the actual attributes of birds, taking advantage of the aggregate human mind and our intrinsic association with the regular world.

The imagery of birds in folklore is huge and multi-layered. Flight, for example, fills in as a strong representation for otherworldly height and greatness. The taking off wings of hawks, the ethereal trip of birds, and the subtle dance of owls in the night sky all add to an emblematic language that rises above social and geological limits. By understanding the nuanced meaning of these images, we gain knowledge into the social qualities, otherworldly yearnings, and cosmological points of view of various social orders.

2. The Inescapability of Birds in Folklore

Why birds? What is it about these padded animals that has driven societies across the globe to hoist them to the situation with divine creatures or intense images? The response lies in the general human experience of noticing birds in flight — superb, free, and apparently untethered to the everyday worries of natural presence. Birds consume a liminal space between the earthbound and the heavenly, epitomizing a feeling of opportunity that has spellbound the human creative mind since days of yore.

Whether it's the consecrated ibis of antiquated Egypt, the mythic Thunderbird of Local American practices, or the exquisite crane in East Asian old stories, birds have been woven into the actual texture of folklore as specialists of creation, shrewdness, and profound direction. The variety of avian imagery across societies prompts us to address whether there is an innate human propensity to look for significance in the normal world and, specifically, in the remarkable trip of birds.

3. Reason and Extent of the Book

"Wings of Godlikeness" isn't simply an investigation of legendary stories yet an undertaking to uncover the hidden human driving forces that have prompted the formation of avian divinities in different societies. Through an interdisciplinary methodology that draws from folklore, religion, human sciences, and biology, this book tries to give a far reaching comprehension of the jobs birds have played in forming human conviction frameworks, social personalities, and profound practices.

The extent of our investigation reaches out across landmasses and ages, from the banks of the Nile to the islands of the Pacific, from old looks to contemporary writing and craftsmanship. By inspecting the common themes and subjects encompassing avian gods, we intend to enlighten the common human encounters that rise above the limits of time and geology. Through this excursion, we welcome perusers to think about the significant manners by which our interconnectedness with the normal world, as represented by the trip of birds, has formed the woven artwork of human culture.

In the parts that follow, we will dive into the particular avian divinities of old developments, investigating their legends, imagery, and social importance. We will unwind the strings that interface birds to creation legends, strict texts, and the idea of creature symbols. Also, we will examine the jobs of birds in fighting, shrewdness customs, and their advanced variations in writing, workmanship, and mainstream society.

As we explore this tremendous and multifaceted scene, "Wings of Divine nature" welcomes perusers to leave on an otherworldly excursion — a trip of the human soul through the rich embroidery of avian folklore. In doing as such, we desire to enlighten not just the different convictions and stories encompassing avian divinities yet in addition the general human mission for importance, association, and the timeless appeal of the skies.

A.   Definition and significance of avian deities

Birds, with their rich flight and charming presence, have risen above their natural presence to become images of the heavenly in different societies across the globe. Implanted inside the texture of folklore, these winged animals have accepted the responsibility of divinities, going about as couriers, watchmen, and encapsulations of enormous powers. To comprehend the profundity of this peculiarity, it is fundamental to investigate the definition and meaning of avian divinities — the otherworldly substances that span the domains of the natural and the heavenly.

Characterizing Avian Divinities:

The expression "avian divinities" alludes to divine creatures or substances that either appear as birds or have critical avian characteristics. Dissimilar to human gods that bear human-like characteristics, avian divinities manifest the heavenly in a structure that mirrors the normal world, explicitly the spectacular and powerful nature of birds. This sign can go from divine beings with bird-like highlights to birds raised to the situation with holy couriers or images of amazing quality.

In the pantheon of avian divinities, one frequently experiences creatures that are crossovers — obscuring the lines between the avian and the human. Consider, for example, the old Egyptian god Horus, portrayed with the top of a bird of prey, representing both the heavenly and the taking off soul of the hawk. Essentially, in Hindu folklore, Garuda, a legendary bird and mount of the god Vishnu, exemplifies both avian beauty and heavenly strength.

Past these human portrayals, avian gods can likewise appear as spirits or powers dwelling inside birds. This type of indication frequently features the interconnectedness between the normal world and the heavenly. The old Greeks, for instance, trusted in the meaning of birds as couriers of the divine beings. The owl, related with the goddess Athena, represented astuteness, while hawks were thought of as holy to Zeus, the ruler of the divine beings.

The Meaning of Avian Divinities:

The height of birds to the situation with gods helps significant importance that reverberates through the social, otherworldly, and emblematic elements of human life.

1. Couriers of the Heavenly:

Birds, with their capacity to navigate the skies, have been seen as couriers between the natural and heavenly domains. In numerous folklores, they act as conductors for correspondence among divine beings and humans. The scriptural story of Noah's Ark, for example, includes a bird sent by Noah to track down land — an image of trust and heavenly direction.

The theme of courier birds isn't bound to Western customs; it penetrates the stories of different societies, underlining the general human interest with birds as middle people with the heavenly.

2. Images of Opportunity and Amazing quality:
The imagery of flight is innate in the pith of birds, and it reverberates profoundly in the human mind. Avian divinities, frequently connected with flight, become images of opportunity and greatness. In old Greek folklore, the winged shoes of Hermes, the courier god, permitted him to navigate huge distances in a matter of moments, underlining the freeing force of flight. Birds taking off through the sky inspire a feeling of otherworldly rise, addressing the human goal to rise above natural restrictions.

3. Gatekeepers and Defenders:
Numerous avian gods take on jobs as gatekeepers or defenders, typifying characteristics like strength, carefulness, and intelligence. The idea of creature emblems, predominant in native societies, frequently connects explicit birds with defensive spirits. In Local American customs, the Thunderbird is a strong and big-hearted force, representing security and help from above. The owl, with its nighttime shrewdness, is venerated as a watchman in different societies, from old Greece to Local American fables.

4. Creation and Ripeness Images:
Birds are habitually connected to creation fantasies and richness imagery. In old Egyptian folklore, the ibis, related with the god Thoth, represented imagination and shrewdness. The peacock, with its lively plumage, is an image of excellence, richness, and revival in Hindu and Greek legends. The association among birds and creation highlights the confidence in the invigorating characteristics of these animals and their part in the patterns of nature.

5. Impressions of Social Qualities:
The decision of explicit birds as divinities reflects social qualities and cultural beliefs. For instance, in Japanese fables, the crane is an image of life span and favorable luck, typifying qualities like steadfastness and devotion. The relationship of explicit birds with specific excellencies or traits gives knowledge into the qualities maintained by various social orders, offering a brief look into the social embroidery woven around avian divinities.

6. Respect for Nature:
The exaltation of birds in different societies underscores a significant veneration for the normal world.

Avian divinities frequently act as middle people among divine beings and people as well as among humankind and the more extensive biological system. The entwining of the heavenly with the regular world highlights the natural association among otherworldliness and the climate, encouraging a feeling of environmental cognizance.

B.   The pervasive role of birds in mythology

Birds, with their ethereal flights and dazzling tunes, have been woven into the texture of human folklore since days of yore. Across different societies and ages, these winged animals play played multi-layered parts, filling in as images of heavenliness, couriers of the divine beings, and allegories for the human condition. The unavoidable job of birds in folklore rises above geological limits, mirroring a common human interest with the avian world and its significant emblematic importance.

1. Birds as Couriers of the Heavenly:

One of the most common jobs alloted to birds in folklore is that of couriers between the natural and heavenly domains. The capacity of birds to cross tremendous distances, taking off through the sky, has driven many societies to consider them to be channels for correspondence with the divine beings. In Greek folklore, the owl, holy to the goddess Athena, represented shrewdness and filled in as her courier. Additionally, the antiquated Egyptians trusted that birds, especially the ibis, conveyed messages from the divine beings to the human domain.

This subject isn't bound to Western practices. In Hindu folklore, the Garuda, a legendary bird and mount of the god Vishnu, is a guardian angel related with the conveyance of significant messages among divine beings and people. The idea of birds as couriers is unavoidable, mirroring a widespread human craving for a connection between the unmistakable and the heavenly, where the trip of birds turns into a similitude for otherworldly greatness.

2. Imagery of Flight and Opportunity:

The actual pith of birds — their capacity to take off — makes them powerful images of opportunity and greatness. The picture of a bird taking off through the open sky has reverberated with human societies across the globe as a portrayal of freedom from natural limitations. In antiquated Greek folklore, Icarus and his waxen wings epitomize the human longing to get away from the natural domain and reach for the sky. The thought of trip as a similitude for the human soul's longing to break liberated from constraints tracks down articulation in endless fantasies and stories.

In Local American societies, the falcon is an image of opportunity and boldness, venerated for its capacity to fly at extraordinary levels. The superb spread of its wings turns into an image of the broad vistas that the human soul tries to investigate.

Likewise, in Chinese folklore, the phoenix addresses the pattern of death and resurrection, with its flight encapsulating the never-ending restoration of life and the otherworldly idea of the spirit.

3. Birds as Mediators Between Domains:
Past filling in as couriers, birds frequently go about as delegates between various domains — overcoming any issues between the natural and the otherworldly, the ordinary and the heavenly. In Norse folklore, ravens are related with the god Odin and are accepted to bring him data from the human domain. Huginn and Muninn, Odin's ravens, fly across the world and return to murmur mysteries into the god's ear, underlining the association between the heavenly and the regular.
In different shamanic customs, birds are viewed as advisers for supernatural domains. The idea of the "soul bird" is predominant in societies like the antiquated Egyptians and the native people groups of North America, where birds are remembered to convey the spirit on its excursion in the afterlife. The imagery of birds as mediators highlights their job as profound aides, working with changes between various conditions.

4. Avian Gods in Creation Legends:
Birds oftentimes highlight noticeably in creation fantasies, epitomizing the imaginative powers that shape the universe. The demonstration of flight becomes inseparable from the demonstration of creation, as birds explore the heavenly region, forming the world and its occupants. In old Egyptian folklore, the early stage goose laid the vast egg, from which the sun god Ra arose. The imagery of the egg, combined with the bird's relationship with the sun, embodies subjects of creation, ripeness, and enormous request.
Additionally, in Greek folklore, the singing of birds is entwined with the making of the world. The alarms, frequently portrayed with bird-like highlights, are legendary creatures whose captivating melodies added to the arrangement of the universe. Birds, in these fantasies, are not detached eyewitnesses but rather dynamic members in the unfurling of the universe.

5. Birds as Images of Insight and Information:
The relationship among birds and shrewdness is a repetitive theme in folklore, rising above social limits. The owl, with its nighttime watchfulness and sharp detects, has been an image of shrewdness in old Greek and Roman societies, as well as in Hindu folklore. The goddess Athena, frequently portrayed with an owl, epitomizes the combination of shrewdness and avian imagery.
In Norse folklore, the ravens Huginn and Muninn, related with Odin, address thought and memory, underlining the job of birds as transporters of information.

Birds having bits of knowledge outside human ability to understand mirrors a confidence in the natural insight implanted in the regular world.

6. Birds in Representative Duality:
Birds frequently typify dualistic characteristics, addressing both positive and negative powers, life and passing, creation and obliteration. In old Mesopotamian folklore, the Anzû bird is a complicated figure, representing both the force of tempests and the potential for restoration. Essentially, the idea of the thunderbird in Local American practices conveys both good and unfortunate underlying meanings, representing both nurturing precipitation and horrendous tempests.
This dualistic imagery is likewise obvious in the figure of the phoenix, a legendary bird that consistently recovers through fire. The phoenix's capacity to ascend from its own remains addresses the groundbreaking force of obliteration and recharging — a subject that resounds across different societies and legends.

7. Birds in Customs and Emblematic Practices:
The emblematic meaning of birds stretches out past folklore and pervades social customs and representative practices. In old Rome, for instance, forecasts deciphered the flight examples and calls of birds to anticipate the future — an old practice known as soothsaying. The idea of perusing signs from birds isn't restricted to Western societies; it is likewise tracked down in different structures in Chinese, Hindu, and native customs. The utilization of birds in ceremonies highlights their apparent capacity to impart messages from the profound domain. Quills, homes, and other avian components are integrated into stylized works on, filling in as channels for profound energy and heavenly favors. The customs including birds further feature the cozy association among people and the avian world, rising above the limits of fantasy and entering the domain of lived social practices.

C.   Purpose and scope of the book
In the tremendous embroidery of human folklore, hardly any images have held as significant and general a spot as birds. "Wings of Eternality" tries to disentangle the secrets woven into the plumes of these winged animals, investigating their jobs as avian divinities and images across societies and ages. The reason for this book is complex, meaning to enlighten the common human interest with birds while looking at the assorted manners by which societies have instilled them with mythic importance.

1. Enlightening the All inclusive Human Association with Birds:
The basic role of "Wings of Eternality" is to enlighten the all inclusive human association with birds. Birds, with their capacity to take off through the skies, have caught the creative mind of individuals across the globe.

The book looks to dig into the purposes for this interest, investigating how birds, from the great hawk to the enchanted phoenix, rise above social and geological limits to become images of the heavenly and specialists of amazing quality.

By understanding the widespread allure of birds, the book plans to unwind the ongoing ideas that join mankind in its veneration for these animals. Whether in the old legends of Egypt or the fables of native clans, birds have filled in as couriers, images of opportunity, and epitomes of enormous powers. The object is to uncover the model components that continue across societies, uncovering the inborn human association with the regular world and the divine domains.

2. Spanning Old Insight with Current Points of view:

The extent of "Wings of Heavenly nature" reaches out across transient limits, making a scaffold between old insight and present day points of view. While diving into the folklores of human advancements like Egypt, Greece, and India, the book additionally investigates contemporary translations of avian imagery in writing, workmanship, and mainstream society. This double investigation effectively shows the persevering through importance of avian divinities in forming social stories and articulations.

By embracing both the antiquated and the advanced, the book looks to exhibit the ageless idea of avian imagery. It digs into how the subjects woven into legends from centuries prior keep on reverberating in the present stories, featuring the persevering through effect of birds on the human creative mind. The design isn't just to figure out the verifiable underlying foundations of avian divinities yet additionally to observe their proceeded with advancement in the unique scene of contemporary idea and imagination.

3. Comprehensive Interdisciplinary Investigation:

"Wings of Heavenly nature" embraces an interdisciplinary way to deal with give perusers a comprehensive investigation of avian divinities. Past folklore, the book draws experiences from human studies, religion, environment, and writing to enhance the comprehension of the jobs birds play in forming social personalities. This interdisciplinary focal point considers a thorough assessment of the complex associations among birds and human societies.

For instance, the book digs into the environmental viewpoints on birds, taking into account the effect of human connections on avian species and the more extensive ramifications for the normal world. This investigation is entwined with the emblematic and otherworldly elements of birds, offering perusers a nuanced comprehension of the multifaceted connection among people and the avian world. The intention is to introduce a far reaching story that rises above customary disciplinary limits, welcoming perusers to draw in with avian imagery according to different points of view.

4. Investigating Social Variety and Subtlety:

The extent of "Wings of Heavenliness" embraces the rich variety and subtlety encompassing avian gods in various societies. From the sacrosanct ibis in antiquated Egypt to the Thunderbird in Local American customs, each culture implants its avian imagery with remarkable implications, mirroring its qualities, cosmology, and otherworldly convictions. The book expects to commend this variety while uncovering the basic subjects that reverberate across societies.

By investigating avian gods in old civilizations and native societies, the book welcomes perusers to see the value in the social wealth implanted in avian imagery. The design isn't just to feature the novel articulations of each culture yet in addition to perceive the ongoing ideas that join mankind in its interest with these winged animals. In doing as such, the book cultivates social education and appreciation, empowering perusers to investigate the unpredictable embroidery of worldwide legends.

5. Natural Mindfulness and Preservation Points of view:

Past folklore, "Wings of Heavenly nature" likewise consolidates an ecological mindfulness and protection viewpoint. The reason this is to investigate the way social view of birds converge with contemporary environmental difficulties. By analyzing the manners by which birds are adored, secured, or took advantage of in various social settings, the book plans to reveal insight into the perplexing connection among people and avian species.

This ecological viewpoint upgrades how we might interpret avian divinities inside their social settings, provoking reflection on the obligation people bear in safeguarding the normal world. By interlacing folklore with natural contemplations, the book tries to move a restored appreciation for the many-sided trap of life that incorporates both the representative and unmistakable parts of the avian domain. The intention is to overcome any barrier between social accounts and natural cognizance, empowering perusers to perceive the interconnectedness of social and biological scenes.

6. Cultivating Multifaceted Exchange:

One general motivation behind "Wings of Divine nature" is to encourage diverse exchange. By welcoming perusers to investigate avian divinities from different societies, the book makes a space for social trade and common comprehension. It urges perusers to see the value in the similitudes and contrasts in how various social orders conceptualize and respect birds, consequently adding to a more extensive discussion about the comprehensiveness of human encounters.

The extent of the book works with an investigation of social convergences, permitting perusers to draw associations between apparently unique folklores and uncover shared subjects that cross social limits.

In doing as such, "Wings of Heavenliness" turns into an impetus for advancing social education and appreciation in an undeniably interconnected worldwide scene. The object is to develop a feeling of shared mankind, rising above contrasts and praising the different articulations of the human creative mind.

Chapter 1
The Bird as Symbol

The bird, with its wings spread wide, has for quite some time been an insignia of greatness, opportunity, and the ethereal. In societies around the world, this avian animal has woven itself into the representative embroidery of human life. From the heavenly trips of legendary divinities to the unassuming sparrows gracing our regular day to day existences, the bird fills in as a strong image wealthy in different implications. In this investigation, we adventure into the significant and multi-layered domain of the bird as an image, navigating societies, folklores, religions, and contemporary understandings.

I. The Illustration of Flight:
A. Opportunity and Freedom:
Old Greece and Winged Shoes: In old Greek folklore, the god Hermes is frequently portrayed with winged shoes, representing his job as a courier and guide. The wings, empowering quick and light-footed flight, encapsulate the opportunity to navigate domains and convey messages among divine beings and humans.

Local American Thunderbird: Across Local American societies, the Thunderbird is a strong image related with tempests. Its capacity to take off through the skies addresses an association between the natural and the otherworldly, epitomizing the opportunity to move between domains.

Chinese Folklore - Fenghuang (Phoenix): The phoenix, a legendary bird in Chinese folklore, represents restoration and recharging. Its cyclic passing and resurrection build up the possibility of independence from the requirements of mortality and the timeless pattern of life.

B. Profound Rise:
Norse Folklore - Huginn and Muninn: In Norse folklore, Odin's ravens, Huginn (thought) and Muninn (memory), take off through the domains, bringing back data. Their flight addresses the profound rise of thought and memory, interfacing the natural with the heavenly.

Hindu Garuda: In Hindu folklore, Garuda, a legendary falcon, is the mount of Master Vishnu. Garuda's capacity to fly at extraordinary rates connotes profound climb, accentuating the spirit's excursion towards higher awareness.

Sufi Supernatural quality - The Simurgh: In Persian writing and Sufi enchantment, the Simurgh, a legendary bird, addresses the spirit's excursion towards self-revelation and heavenly association. The bird's flight turns into a similitude for rising above oneself and arriving at otherworldly levels.

C. Journey for Information:
Greek Owl of Athena: The owl, image of astuteness, is related with the Greek goddess Athena. Its nighttime flight connotes the mission for information and the quest for astuteness in the haziness of obliviousness.

Local American Owl: Likewise, in Local American societies, the owl is an image of shrewdness and instinct. Its quiet flight is viewed as an aide through the concealed domains, enlightening the way to information.

Egyptian Ibis - Thoth: The old Egyptians venerated the ibis, especially connected with the god Thoth, as an image of shrewdness and information. Thoth's holy ibis encapsulates the trip of intelligence from the heavenly to the human domain.

II. Birds as Couriers of the Heavenly:
A. Scriptural Imagery:

Noah's Pigeon: In the Book of scriptures, the bird assumes a vital part in the narrative of Noah's Ark. Conveyed to find land after the flood, the pigeon's return with a peace offering turns into an image of trust and heavenly correspondence.

Essence of God as Bird: In Christian imagery, the pigeon is frequently connected with the Essence of God. Its appearance during critical scriptural occasions, like Jesus' submersion, highlights the bird's job as a guardian angel.

B. Hindu Folklore - Swan (Hamsa):
In Hindu folklore, the swan (Hamsa) is an image of immaculateness and profound elegance. It is frequently connected with the goddess Saraswati, addressing the acumen expected to isolate truth from deception.

Hindu Transporter Birds (Suparna): Different legendary birds, like Suparna, act as transporters for divinities in Hindu folklore. Their flight represents the heavenly association between the natural and divine domains.

C. Mesopotamian Winged Creatures:
Assyrian Winged Bulls and Divine beings: In Mesopotamian craftsmanship, winged bulls and divinities are predominant, representing heavenly security and strength. Their wings mean the heavenly nature and their job as middle people between the human and heavenly universes.

Sumerian Anzu Bird: The Anzu bird, portrayed in Sumerian folklore, is a heavenly being frequently connected with shrewdness. Its wings address the divine idea of the bird and its job in conveying messages between divine beings.

III. Birds in Creation Fantasies:
A. Egyptian Ibis - Thoth and the Enormous Egg:
In old Egyptian folklore, Thoth, frequently portrayed as an ibis, is related with the making of the world. The ibis' job in molding the enormous egg connotes the bird's contribution in the actual texture of creation.

Greek Phoenix and Enormous Cycles: The phoenix in Greek folklore, consistently recovering through fire, addresses the everlasting patterns of creation and annihilation. Its departure from cinders to new life embodies the subject of enormous restoration.

B. Chinese Fenghuang (Phoenix):
In Chinese folklore, the Fenghuang, much the same as the phoenix, represents the amicable association of alternate extremes. Its flight implies the equilibrium between yin and yang, adding to astronomical request and the propagation of life.

Norse Bird and Creation Fantasy: In Norse folklore, a falcon sits at the highest point of Yggdrasil, the world tree, supervising creation. Its departure from the most noteworthy branches to the human domain means the steady progression of life and presence.

C. Maya Quetzal Bird:*
In Maya folklore, the quetzal bird is related with the making of mankind. Its bright plumage and exquisite flight are representative of the magnificence and variety woven into the texture of presence.

Hopi Sun Soul: Among the Hopi public, the sun soul, frequently addressed as a bird, assumes a focal part in creation legends. The bird's trip across the sky reflects the excursion of the sun and the unfurling of life.

IV. Birds as Images of Dualities:
A. Mesopotamian Anzu Bird:
The Anzu bird in Mesopotamian folklore addresses both turmoil and revival. Its wings, representing the force of tempests, are dualistic, exemplifying both the damaging powers of nature and the potential for reestablishment.

Local American Thunderbird: The Thunderbird, pervasive in different Local American societies, represents both nurturing precipitation and disastrous tempests. Its double nature reflects the patterns of creation and obliteration innate in the regular world.

B. Greek Alarms and the Vagueness of Flight:
The alarms in Greek folklore, frequently portrayed with bird-like highlights, encapsulate the double idea of their captivating melodies. Their flight and charm are both enrapturing and unsafe, addressing the vagueness of the avian image.

Japanese Tengu: In Japanese fables, the Tengu is a legendary animal with both bird and human credits. It encapsulates dualities, addressing both big-hearted and malicious powers in nature.

C. Emblematic Duality in Chinese Fenghuang (Phoenix):
The Fenghuang in Chinese folklore typifies the duality of yin and yang. Its flight represents the agreeable association of alternate extremes, mirroring the sensitive equilibrium essential for infinite request and recharging.

Dualistic Imagery in Hindu Garuda: Garuda, the legendary bird in Hindu folklore, serves both as a mount for Ruler Vishnu and a devourer of snakes. Its double jobs represent the harmony between divine bondage and the important annihilation of enormous snags.

V. Social Variety in Avian Imagery:
A. Japanese Crane (Tsuru):
In Japanese fables, the crane (Tsuru) is an image of life span and favorable luck. Its smooth flight and unmistakable appearance make it a social seal, frequently portrayed in craftsmanship and writing.

Egyptian Hawk (Horus): The bird of prey, related with the god Horus in old Egypt, represents both heavenly assurance and the sharp visual perception required for profound understanding. Its social importance stretches out to the many-sided symbolic representations of antiquated Egyptian composition.

B. Roman Hawk and Royal Imagery:
The falcon, an image of force and authority, assumed an essential part in old Rome. As the norm of the Roman armies, its flight epitomized the development of the domain and the could of the Roman state.

Maori Tui Bird: Among the Maori nation of New Zealand, the Tui bird is loved for its melodic tunes and dynamic plumage. Its flight is emblematic of the otherworldly association between the natural and heavenly domains.

C. Emblematic Varieties in Local American Customs:
Hopi Parrot Katsina: Among the Hopi public, the parrot is related with Katsinam, otherworldly creatures that exemplify normal components. The bird's flight turns into an illustration for the repetitive idea of life and the interconnectedness, everything being equal.

Inuit Raven: In Inuit folklore, the raven is a complex image, exemplifying both creation and fraud. Its trip across the Cold skies mirrors the duality of its temperament and its fundamental job in Inuit social accounts.

VI. Birds in Contemporary Imagery:
A. Opportunity in Current Settings:
In contemporary writing and craftsmanship, the imagery of birds as specialists of opportunity perseveres. Books as bach Richard's "Jonathan Livingston Seagull" and films like "The Birdman of Alcatraz" investigate the topic of individual freedom and amazing quality through the similitude of flight.

Harmony Pigeon in Activism: The bird, an image of harmony, stays common in current activism. From hostile to war fights to natural developments, the bird's flight keeps on addressing the yearnings for an amicable and freed world.

B. Mechanical Flight and Advancement:
In the cutting edge period, the allegory of flight has stretched out past the regular domain. Planes, robots, and space investigation represent humankind's quest for mechanical development and the journey to vanquish new boondocks.

Space Investigation and Grandiose Flight: The symbolism of birds in space investigation logos, like NASA's notorious seal, mirrors a contemporary understanding of avian imagery. Birds, in this specific circumstance, become images of mankind's desire to investigate the universe.

C. Natural Mindfulness:
As natural worries develop, birds become images of biological equilibrium and the sensitive interconnectedness of environments. Preservation endeavors frequently use birds as ministers for more extensive ecological mindfulness.

Birdwatching and Nature Association: In the cutting edge setting, birdwatching has arisen as a famous sporting movement, underlining the remedial and profound parts of interfacing with nature. The trip of birds turns into a wellspring of motivation and consideration for fans.

1.1   Birds as messengers of the divine

The bird, with its wings spread wide, has for some time been an image of greatness, opportunity, and the ethereal. In societies around the world, this avian animal has woven itself into the emblematic embroidery of human life. From the divine trips of legendary divinities to the modest sparrows gracing our daily existences, the bird fills in as a powerful image wealthy in different implications. In this investigation, we adventure into the significant and multi-layered domain of the bird as an image, navigating societies, folklores, religions, and contemporary understandings.

I. The Allegory of Flight:
A. Opportunity and Freedom:

Old Greece and Winged Shoes: In old Greek folklore, the god Hermes is frequently portrayed with winged shoes, representing his job as a courier and guide. The wings, empowering quick and nimble flight, typify the opportunity to navigate domains and convey messages among divine beings and humans.

Local American Thunderbird: Across Local American societies, the Thunderbird is a strong image related with rainstorms. Its capacity to take off through the skies addresses an association between the natural and the profound, encapsulating the opportunity to move between domains.

Chinese Folklore - Fenghuang (Phoenix): The phoenix, a legendary bird in Chinese folklore, represents revival and restoration. Its cyclic demise and resurrection build up the possibility of independence from the requirements of mortality and the timeless pattern of life.

B. Otherworldly Rise:
Norse Folklore - Huginn and Muninn: In Norse folklore, Odin's ravens, Huginn (thought) and Muninn (memory), take off through the domains, bringing back data.

Their flight addresses the otherworldly rise of thought and memory, interfacing the natural with the heavenly.

Hindu Garuda: In Hindu folklore, Garuda, a legendary bird, is the mount of Ruler Vishnu. Garuda's capacity to fly at extraordinary paces connotes profound rising, underlining the spirit's excursion towards higher cognizance.

Sufi Enchantment - The Simurgh: In Persian writing and Sufi magic, the Simurgh, a legendary bird, addresses the spirit's excursion towards self-disclosure and heavenly association. The bird's flight turns into a similitude for rising above oneself and arriving at profound levels.

C. Mission for Information:
Greek Owl of Athena: The owl, image of insight, is related with the Greek goddess Athena. Its nighttime flight means the mission for information and the quest for shrewdness in the obscurity of obliviousness.

Local American Owl: Likewise, in Local American societies, the owl is an image of shrewdness and instinct. Its quiet flight is viewed as an aide through the concealed domains, enlightening the way to information.

Egyptian Ibis - Thoth: The old Egyptians respected the ibis, especially connected with the god Thoth, as an image of shrewdness and information. Thoth's hallowed ibis epitomizes the trip of intelligence from the heavenly to the human domain.

II. Birds as Couriers of the Heavenly:
A. Scriptural Imagery:

Noah's Pigeon: In the Good book, the bird assumes a urgent part in the tale of Noah's Ark. Conveyed to find land after the flood, the bird's return with a peace offering turns into an image of trust and heavenly correspondence.

Essence of God as Bird: In Christian imagery, the pigeon is frequently connected with the Essence of God. Its appearance during critical scriptural occasions, like Jesus' submersion, highlights the bird's job as a guardian angel.

B. Hindu Folklore - Swan (Hamsa):
In Hindu folklore, the swan (Hamsa) is an image of immaculateness and otherworldly elegance. It is frequently connected with the goddess Saraswati, addressing the insight expected to isolate truth from lie.

Hindu Transporter Birds (Suparna): Different legendary birds, like Suparna, act as transporters for gods in Hindu folklore. Their flight represents the heavenly association between the natural and divine domains.

C. Mesopotamian Winged Creatures:
Assyrian Winged Bulls and Divine beings: In Mesopotamian workmanship, winged bulls and gods are predominant, representing heavenly assurance and strength. Their wings imply the heavenly nature and their job as middle people between the human and heavenly universes.

Sumerian Anzu Bird: The Anzu bird, portrayed in Sumerian folklore, is a heavenly being frequently connected with shrewdness. Its wings address the divine idea of the bird and its part in conveying messages between divine beings.

III. Birds in Creation Fantasies:
A. Egyptian Ibis - Thoth and the Enormous Egg:
In old Egyptian folklore, Thoth, frequently portrayed as an ibis, is related with the making of the world. The ibis' job in forming the astronomical egg implies the bird's association in the actual texture of creation.

Greek Phoenix and Enormous Cycles: The phoenix in Greek folklore, consistently recovering through fire, addresses the timeless patterns of creation and obliteration. Its departure from cinders to new life exemplifies the subject of inestimable reestablishment.

B. Chinese Fenghuang (Phoenix):
In Chinese folklore, the Fenghuang, similar to the phoenix, represents the amicable association of alternate extremes. Its flight connotes the equilibrium between yin and yang, adding to infinite request and the propagation of life.

Norse Hawk and Creation Fantasy: In Norse folklore, a falcon sits at the highest point of Yggdrasil, the world tree, supervising creation. Its departure from the most elevated branches to the human domain connotes the consistent progression of life and presence.

C. Maya Quetzal Bird:*
In Maya folklore, the quetzal bird is related with the production of humanity. Its vivid plumage and exquisite flight are emblematic of the magnificence and variety woven into the texture of presence.

Hopi Sun Soul: Among the Hopi public, the sun soul, frequently addressed as a bird, assumes a focal part in creation fantasies. The bird's trip across the sky reflects the excursion of the sun and the unfurling of life.

IV. Birds as Images of Dualities:
A. Mesopotamian Anzu Bird:
The Anzu bird in Mesopotamian folklore addresses both mayhem and revival. Its wings, representing the force of tempests, are dualistic, exemplifying both the disastrous powers of nature and the potential for recharging.

Local American Thunderbird: The Thunderbird, predominant in different Local American societies, represents both nurturing precipitation and horrendous tempests. Its double nature reflects the patterns of creation and annihilation intrinsic in the regular world.

B. Greek Alarms and the Vagueness of Flight:
The alarms in Greek folklore, frequently portrayed with bird-like highlights, typify the double idea of their captivating melodies. Their flight and appeal are both spellbinding and dangerous, addressing the equivocalness of the avian image.

Japanese Tengu: In Japanese legends, the Tengu is a legendary animal with both bird and human credits. It typifies dualities, addressing both generous and malignant powers in nature.

C. Representative Duality in Chinese Fenghuang (Phoenix):
The Fenghuang in Chinese folklore encapsulates the duality of yin and yang. Its flight represents the agreeable association of contrary energies, mirroring the sensitive equilibrium essential for inestimable request and recharging.

Dualistic Imagery in Hindu Garuda: Garuda, the legendary falcon in Hindu folklore, serves both as a mount for Master Vishnu and a devourer of snakes. Its double jobs represent the harmony between divine subjugation and the vital obliteration of enormous obstructions.

V. Social Variety in Avian Imagery:
A. Japanese Crane (Tsuru):
In Japanese old stories, the crane (Tsuru) is an image of life span and favorable luck. Its effortless flight and particular appearance make it a social token, frequently portrayed in workmanship and writing.

Egyptian Hawk (Horus): The bird of prey, related with the god Horus in old Egypt, represents both heavenly assurance and the sharp visual perception required for otherworldly knowledge. Its social importance reaches out to the multifaceted symbolic representations of old Egyptian composition.

B. Roman Bird and Majestic Imagery:

The bird, an image of force and authority, assumed a significant part in old Rome. As the norm of the Roman armies, its flight epitomized the development of the realm and the could of the Roman state.

Maori Tui Bird: Among the Maori nation of New Zealand, the Tui bird is venerated for its melodic tunes and dynamic plumage. Its flight is representative of the otherworldly association between the natural and heavenly domains.

C. Representative Varieties in Local American Customs:

Hopi Parrot Katsina: Among the Hopi public, the parrot is related with Katsinam, otherworldly creatures that encapsulate regular components. The bird's flight turns into a representation for the repetitive idea of life and the interconnectedness, everything being equal.

Inuit Raven: In Inuit folklore, the raven is a diverse image, typifying both creation and craftiness. Its trip across the Icy skies mirrors the duality of its temperament and its fundamental job in Inuit social accounts.

VI. Birds in Contemporary Imagery:

A. Opportunity in Present day Settings:

In contemporary writing and workmanship, the imagery of birds as specialists of opportunity perseveres. Books as bach Richard's "Jonathan Livingston Seagull" and motion pictures like "The Birdman of Alcatraz" investigate the topic of individual freedom and amazing quality through the similitude of flight.

Harmony Bird in Activism: The pigeon, an image of harmony, stays pervasive in current activism. From hostile to war fights to natural developments, the bird's flight keeps on addressing the yearnings for an amicable and freed world.

B. Mechanical Flight and Development:

In the advanced period, the illustration of flight has reached out past the regular domain. Planes, robots, and space investigation represent humankind's quest for mechanical development and the mission to overcome new boondocks.

Space Investigation and Vast Flight: The symbolism of birds in space investigation logos, like NASA's notorious seal, mirrors a contemporary understanding of avian imagery. Birds, in this specific situation, become images of mankind's desire to investigate the universe.

C. Natural Mindfulness:
As natural worries develop, birds become images of biological equilibrium and the sensitive interconnectedness of environments. Preservation endeavors frequently use birds as ministers for more extensive ecological mindfulness.

Birdwatching and Nature Association: In the cutting edge setting, birdwatching has arisen as a famous sporting action, underlining the remedial and otherworldly parts of associating with nature. The trip of birds turns into a wellspring of motivation and examination for lovers.

1.2   Symbolism of flight and freedom

The imagery of flight and opportunity reverberates profoundly inside the aggregate human awareness, rising above social, strict, and geological limits. The symbolism of birds taking off, unburdened by the requirements of gravity, has long charmed the human creative mind. This imagery goes past the simple actual demonstration of flying; it addresses a significant representation for freedom, greatness, and the vast possible inborn in the human soul. In this investigation, we dive into the rich layers of imagery related with flight and opportunity, looking at its multi-layered signs across societies and from the beginning of time.

I. Birds as Symbols of Opportunity:
A. Birds as Images of Harmony and Opportunity:

Scriptural Setting: The bird, representing harmony and opportunity, is well established in scriptural stories. Its appearance in the narrative of Noah's Ark addresses the finish of the downpour and the commitment of a fresh start. The pigeon's flight exemplifies the freedom from the waters of tumult.

Christian Imagery: In Christian practices, the pigeon is related with the Essence of God, representing profound opportunity and heavenly direction. The theme of a pigeon conveying a peace offering turned into a persevering through image of harmony, portraying independence from struggle and struggle.

B. Raptors as Images of Sway:
Hawks in Antiquated Societies: Across different societies, falcons are worshipped as images of opportunity and power. In old Rome, the hawk was an image of supreme may, while in Local American customs, it addressed otherworldly power. The hawk's capacity to take off at incredible levels is a representation for rising above natural limits.

Bird of prey and Bird of prey in Native Practices: Among Local American clans, falcons and hawks are viewed as couriers and images of opportunity. Their quick flight and sharp vision represent the quest for one's way with clearness and the freedom of the soul.

II. Trip as an Illustration for Greatness:
A. Legendary Animals and Heavenly Ascendance:

Greek Pegasus: In Greek folklore, Pegasus, the winged pony, encapsulates the idea of trip as heavenly ascendance. Brought into the world from the blood of the Gorgon Medusa, Pegasus represents the otherworldly power that rises up out of testing conditions.

Hindu Garuda: In Hindu folklore, Garuda, a legendary falcon, fills in as the mount of Ruler Vishnu. Garuda's flight addresses the otherworldly climb of the spirit, underscoring the potential for greatness past common requirements.

B. Winged Gods and Otherworldly Freedom:
Egyptian Ba-Bird: In antiquated Egyptian convictions, the Ba-bird is frequently portrayed with wings, representing the spirit's excursion into life following death. The trip of the Ba-bird connotes profound freedom and the progress to a higher plane of presence.

Mesopotamian Winged Creatures: In Mesopotamian craftsmanship, winged creatures are predominant, filling in as delegates between the heavenly and mortal domains. These portrayals highlight the emblematic meaning of trip for of associating with the consecrated.

III. Trip as Freedom from Natural Limitations:
A. Inflatables and Carriers in Human Advancement:

Verifiable Investigation: The creation of inflatables and aircrafts stamped huge achievements in human development. The capacity to climb into the skies represented freedom from the limits of the Earth, empowering investigation and a more extensive point of view on the world.

Current Aeronautics: The advancement of planes in the twentieth century changed the emblematic significance of flight. Air travel turned into an illustration for the freedom of reality, interfacing far off corners of the globe and encouraging a feeling of worldwide interconnectedness.

B. Bug Trip as an Image of Transformation:
Dragonflies and Butterflies: In the normal world, the trip of bugs like dragonflies and butterflies is representative of versatility and change. These animals go through transformation, shedding the limitations of their previous structures and embracing a newly discovered opportunity in flight.

Honey bees and Aggregate Opportunity: Honey bees, through their organized flight designs, represent aggregate opportunity and amicability. Every honey bee adds to the aggregate reason, stressing the interconnected idea of opportunity inside a local area.

IV. Freedom in Scholarly and Creative Articulation:
A. Scholarly Investigation of Flight:

Scholarly Symbolism: All through writing, flight fills in as a strong similitude for freedom and self-revelation. From Icarus' disastrous trip in Greek folklore to Jonathan Livingston Seagull's journey for profound opportunity in Richard Bach's novella, creators have involved trip as a scholarly gadget to investigate subjects of greatness.

Imagery in Verse: Artists frequently utilize bird symbolism and flight imagery to convey subjects of opportunity and the human soul's ability to take off above difficulty. Pablo Neruda's "Bird" and Maya Angelou's "I Know Why the Confined Bird Sings" embody this emblematic investigation.

B. Creative Portrayals of Flight:
Renaissance Craftsmanship: During the Renaissance, specialists portrayed heavenly messengers and winged figures in flight, representing help from above and the human soul's ability for amazing quality. Works like Leonardo da Vinci's "The Sanctification of Christ" represent the imaginative investigation of flight.

Surrealist Workmanship: In the twentieth hundred years, surrealists like René Magritte and Salvador Dalí integrated flight imagery into their works, provoking customary viewpoints and welcoming watchers to consider the limits among the real world and creative mind.

V. Trip as a Political and Social Illustration:
A. Imagery in Political Developments:

Tranquil Opposition: The demonstration of flying kites, as found in developments like India's battle for freedom, turned into an emblematic type of serene obstruction. Kites taking off overhead addressed the craving for freedom from pilgrim rule.

Butterflies in Social equality Developments: In the social liberties development, the butterfly turned into an image of change and opportunity. Craftsmen and activists involved the picture of a butterfly in trip to convey the yearnings for racial correspondence and civil rights.

B. Opportunity of Articulation in Contemporary Craftsmanship:
Road Craftsmanship and Paintings: Road specialists overall use bird and flight symbolism to impart messages of opportunity, opposition, and trust. Paintings portraying taking off birds act as visual allegories for breaking liberated from cultural limitations.

Establishment Craftsmanship: Contemporary specialists make vivid establishments that investigate the subject of trip as a representation for freedom. These establishments frequently connect with watchers in a multisensory experience, welcoming them to consider the idea of opportunity.

1.3   Birds as intermediaries between realms

Birds have for some time been viewed as mysterious couriers, nimbly exploring the skies and filling in as mediators between the natural and divine domains. This representative job rises above social and strict limits, winding around a consistent idea through different legends and conviction frameworks. In this investigation, we dive into the rich woven artwork of stories and imagery that portray birds as go-betweens, going about as courses for correspondence and greatness between various planes of presence.

I. Avian Couriers in Folklore:
A. Greek Folklore - Courier of the Divine beings:

Hermes and His Winged Shoes: In old Greek folklore, the god Hermes is frequently portrayed with winged shoes, stressing his job as a courier. The quick flight empowered by these shoes represents the heavenly capacity to cross domains and convey messages among divine beings and humans.

Iris, the Rainbow Courier: One more figure in Greek folklore, Iris, is frequently depicted with wings and a rainbow, representing her job as a courier between the sky and Earth. Her trip across the sky reflects the association between the heavenly and the human.

B. Norse Folklore - Odin's Ravens:
Huginn and Muninn: In Norse folklore, the god Odin is joined by two ravens, Huginn (thought) and Muninn (memory). These ravens take off across the domains to accumulate data and take it back to Odin, going about as middle people between the natural and heavenly domains.

World Tree Association: The ravens' relationship with Yggdrasil, the world tree, further highlights their job as couriers interfacing various domains. Their flights represent the consistent progression of data and intelligence between the domains of divine beings and people.

II. Birds in Strict Imagery:
A. Christian Imagery - Essence of God as Pigeon:

Dove at Jesus' Immersion: In Christian practices, the pigeon is a noticeable image of the Essence of God. The pigeon's plummet during Jesus' sanctification connotes divine endorsement and the presence of the Essence of God. Its flight addresses the association between the heavenly and human circles.

Image of Harmony: The pigeon's relationship with harmony, originating from scriptural stories like Noah's Ark, intensifies its job as a middle person. The trip of the bird with a peace offering brings a message of harmony, overcoming any barrier between divine fury and human compromise.

B. Hindu Folklore - Divine Mounts:
Garuda - Ruler Vishnu's Mount: In Hindu folklore, Garuda, a legendary hawk, fills in as the mount of Master Vishnu. Garuda's flight represents the heavenly association between the natural and divine domains. As a go-between, Garuda assumes a vital part in conveying Vishnu to different domains.

Swan and Saraswati: The swan, frequently connected with the goddess Saraswati, typifies intelligence and immaculateness. Saraswati's mount, the swan's flight, addresses the excursion of information from the heavenly to the human domain, going about as a channel for higher comprehension.

III. Birds in Shamanic Customs:
A. Profound Aides and Couriers:

Bird and Falcon in Local American Societies: In different Local American customs, birds and birds of prey are viewed as profound aides and couriers. Their flight is viewed as an association with the soul world, conveying messages and direction between the physical and magical domains.

Crow and Raven in Shamanism: In shamanic practices, crows and ravens are frequently adored as shape-shifters and couriers. Their flight is accepted to open pathways between various aspects, working with correspondence with spirits and progenitors.

IV. Birds as Images of Progress:
A. Egyptian Imagery - Ba-Bird:

Ba-Bird and The great beyond: In antiquated Egyptian convictions, the ba-bird, frequently portrayed with wings, is related with the spirit's excursion into the hereafter. The trip of the ba-bird represents the change from natural presence to the profound domain.

Image of Change: The ba-bird's flight addresses the groundbreaking idea of death and resurrection, going about as a mediator during the progress starting with one condition of being then onto the next.

B. Japanese Imagery - Tengu:
Tengu as Go-betweens: In Japanese fables, the tengu, frequently portrayed with bird-like elements, are viewed as heavenly creatures and middle people among divine beings and people. Their flight represents the capacity to navigate various domains, offering direction and insurance.

Representatives Between Universes: Tengu, with their avian characteristics, go about as diplomats between the natural and otherworldly planes, typifying the interconnectedness of these domains in Japanese social convictions.

Chapter 2
Avian Deities in Ancient Civilizations

The love and reverence of birds as gods have been vital to the profound texture of antiquated human advancements across the globe. From the lofty falcons of Mesopotamia to the worshipped ibis of old Egypt, avian gods have assumed assorted and huge parts in forming social convictions, strict practices, and fanciful accounts. This investigation crosses the huge scenes of olden times, unwinding the unpredictable stories of avian gods in antiquated developments, revealing insight into the significant associations among humankind and the winged divinities that once taken off through the domains of the old world.

I. Mesopotamian Avian Divinities:
A. Anzu - The Heavenly Tempest Bird:

Legendary Beginning: In Mesopotamian folklore, Anzu, otherwise called the "Heavenly Tempest Bird," is a critical avian divinity. Addressed as a lion-headed falcon, Anzu assumes a focal part in different legends, exemplifying the powers of tempests and tumult.

Imagery of Anzu's Flight: Anzu's flight represents the force of tempests and the releasing of heavenly powers upon the human domain. As a divinity related with climate peculiarities, Anzu's flight was accepted to proclaim the methodology of tempests and precipitation.

B. Ishkur - Divine force of Downpour and Tempests:
Properties and Iconography: Ishkur, the Sumerian lord of downpour and rainstorms, is frequently portrayed with the wings of a falcon. His avian properties associate him to the skies and underline his part in controlling the climate.

Trip as a Wellspring of Life: Ishkur's flight represents the nurturing idea of downpour and the fundamental job of tempests in rural richness. The god's capacity to cross the sky and deliver downpour features the recurrent association among flight and food.

II. Egyptian Avian Gods:
A. Horus - The Bird of prey God:

Image of Heavenly Majesty: In old Egypt, Horus, frequently portrayed as a hawk, is a key god related with sovereignty and the pharaoh's heavenly power. His flight represents the defensive look of the hawk, administering the land and guaranteeing its thriving.

Trip in Legendary Accounts: Horus' flight is unmistakable in fantasies, for example, the "Contendings of Horus and Set," where he takes part in heavenly fights, underlining the heavenly battle for request and the unending enormous equilibrium.

B. Thoth - The Ibis of Astuteness:
Avian Imagery: Thoth, the lord of intelligence and composing, is regularly connected with the ibis, a bird with an unmistakable long mouth. Thoth's avian structure addresses the association among insight and flight, as the ibis takes off through the skies with effortlessness and reason.

Trip as a Conductor for Divine Information: Thoth's flight is representative of the transmission of heavenly information to humankind. As the copyist of the divine beings, his wings convey the insight of the sky, overcoming any issues between the heavenly and natural domains.

III. Greek and Roman Avian Divinities:
A. Eos/Aurora - The First light Goddess:

Avian Imagery: Eos in Greek folklore (Aurora in Roman folklore) is the goddess of the first light, frequently portrayed with wings. Her flight proclaims the appearance of the sun and the beginning of another day.

Trip Across the Sky: Eos' day to day trip across the sky addresses the repeating idea of time and the steady recharging of the day. The wings of the sunrise goddess typify the fleeting yet unending nature of the heavenly domains.

B. Nike - Winged Triumph:
Image of Win: In antiquated Greece, Nike, the goddess of triumph, is frequently portrayed with wings. Her flight represents victorious climb, addressing the triumphant result of fights and contests.

Wings of Perseverance: Nike's flight isn't just an image of triumph yet in addition of perseverance and versatility. The goddess' wings exemplify the soul of defeating difficulties and making progress through resolved exertion.

IV. Hindu Avian Divinities:
A. Garuda - The Legendary Bird:

Mount of Vishnu: Garuda, a legendary bird, fills in as the mount of Ruler Vishnu in Hindu folklore. His wings represent quickness and heavenly strength as he conveys Vishnu across the sky.

Trip as Otherworldly Rising: Garuda's flight isn't only an actual demonstration however an illustration for the spirit's excursion toward profound ascendance. His capacity to take off through the divine domains means the quest for higher awareness and illumination.

B. Suparna - Divine Winged Creatures:
Legendary Presence: In Hindu folklore, different gods are related with winged creatures known as Suparnas. These heavenly animals encapsulate the association between the natural and divine domains.

Winged Couriers: Suparnas, through their flight, go about as couriers among divine beings and humans. Their wings convey divine messages and endowments, working with the trading of otherworldly energy and direction.

V. Chinese Avian Divinities:
A. Fenghuang - The Phoenix:

Image of Reestablishment: The Fenghuang, likened to the phoenix in Western folklore, is an image of recharging and resurrection in Chinese custom. Its departure from cinders to new life epitomizes the repeating idea of creation.

Wings of Enormous Amicability: Fenghuang's wings represent the agreeable equilibrium between yin and yang, adding to inestimable request and the propagation of life. Its flight is a dance of grandiose energies, guaranteeing harmony in the regular world.

B. Jiufeng - Nine Phoenixes:
Fanciful Troupe: Jiufeng, signifying "Nine Phoenixes," is a legendary gathering of heavenly birds in Chinese fables.

Their aggregate flight addresses the agreeable association of divine powers and the multifaceted interaction of infinite energies.

Trip as Heavenly Dance: The trip of Jiufeng is likened to a divine dance, arranged by the inestimable powers they typify. Their synchronized developments represent the interconnectedness of the heavenly domains.

VI. Mayan Avian Divinities:
A. Itzamna - Bird Divinity of Creation:

Maker God: Itzamna, an unmistakable god in Mayan folklore, is frequently connected with birds. As a maker god, Itzamna's flight addresses the heavenly demonstration of molding the universe and delivering life.

Wings of Vast Request: Itzamna's wings are images of infinite request and equilibrium. His flight adds to the concordance of the universe, guaranteeing the harmony of normal powers.

B. Quetzal - Radiant Bird:
Image of Holiness: The quetzal bird is venerated in Mayan culture as an image of godliness. Its flight is viewed as a sign of the heavenly, addressing the excellence and holiness woven into the texture of presence.

Trip in Creation Fantasies: Quetzal's flight is frequently connected with the formation of humanity in Mayan folklore. Its elegant developments represent the perplexing dance of life and the rise of conscious creatures.

VII. Avian Divinities in Native Societies:
A. Thunderbird - Local American Practices:

Image of Force: The Thunderbird is a strong and common image in different Local American societies. Its flight is emblematic of the nurturing precipitation and the powerful tempests that bring both annihilation and reestablishment.

Wings of Change: The Thunderbird's wings epitomize groundbreaking power, mirroring the patterns of creation and obliteration intrinsic in the regular world. Its trip across the skies represents the everlasting dance of infinite powers.

B. Hopi Parrot Katsina:
Image of Nature's Amicability: Among the Hopi public, the parrot is related with Katsinam, profound creatures epitomizing normal components. The parrot's flight turns into an illustration for the repeating idea of life and the interconnectedness, everything being equal.

Winged Courier of Otherworldly Lessons: The parrot's flight conveys the insight of profound lessons, going about as a courier between the natural and profound domains. Its lively plumage represents the variety and excellence inborn in the normal request.

VIII. Avian Divinities in Norse Folklore:
A. Huginn and Muninn - Odin's Ravens:

Guardian angels: Huginn (thought) and Muninn (memory) are ravens related with Odin in Norse folklore. Their trip across the world fills in for of social affair data and conveying messages to the god.

Winged Eyewitnesses of Creation: The ravens' flight is representative of steady perception and information gathering. Their wings convey them from the most noteworthy parts of Yggdrasil, the world tree, to the human domain, encapsulating the ceaseless progression of inestimable insight.

B. Valkyries - Choosers of the Killed:
Winged Fight Ladies: Valkyries, champion ladies in Norse folklore, are frequently portrayed with wings. Their trip across front lines represents the determination of fallen champions to be taken to Valhalla, stressing the amazing quality of mortal presence through gallant deeds.

Wings of Predetermination: Valkyries' wings connote their job as referees of fate. Their flight decides the destinies of fighters, highlighting the association between the natural and heavenly planes in the Norse grandiose request.

2.1 Egyptian mythology: Horus, the falcon-headed god

Egyptian folklore is a rich embroidery woven with a heap of divine beings and goddesses, each with their one of a kind credits and importance. Among these divinities, Horus stands apart as quite possibly of the most noticeable and getting through figure in the antiquated Egyptian pantheon. Frequently portrayed as a bird of prey headed god, Horus assumed a vital part in the folklore and strict convictions of old Egypt, encapsulating both heavenly sovereignty and the everlasting battle among request and disarray.

Starting points and Development of Horus:
Horus' starting points can be followed back to the earliest times of antiquated Egyptian progress, and his love developed over centuries. The name "Horus" is a Greek literal interpretation of the Egyptian word "Heru" or "Haru," signifying "the far off one" or "the one over." The idea of Horus was firmly connected to the majesty and the heavenly power of the pharaohs.
The earliest known reference to Horus traces all the way back to the Predynastic Time frame (c. 5500-3100 BCE), where he was related with the sky and addressed as a bird of prey. Nonetheless, it was during the Early Dynastic Period (c. 3100-2686 BCE) that Horus turned out to be unpredictably attached to the pharaohs and their heavenly right to run the show. The pharaoh was viewed as the living encapsulation of Horus on The planet, guaranteeing the success and security of the realm.

Iconography of Horus:
Horus is usually portrayed as a hawk headed man, representing his association with the sky and his job as a heavenly divinity. The hawk, a flying predator known for its sharp visual perception and great flight, was a fitting image for a divine being related with the sky. In certain portrayals, Horus is displayed with the top of a hawk and the body of a man, while in others, he shows up totally as a bird of prey.
One of the most notable images related with Horus is the "Eye of Horus" or "Wedjat Eye." This image, frequently portrayed as the left eye of Horus, addresses security, recuperating, and illustrious power. The legend behind the Eye of Horus is established in a fanciful story of the god's contention with Set, his uncle, which we will investigate exhaustively later.

The Legendary Story of Horus:
The folklore of Horus is complicated and ranges various times of Egyptian history. One of the focal stories includes the contention among Horus and Set, his uncle, for the lofty position of Egypt. This battle addresses the timeless fight between request (Horus) and bedlam (Set) and has profound emblematic importance in Egyptian cosmology.
As indicated by legend, Osiris, the dad of Horus, was the first leader of Egypt. Be that as it may, Osiris was killed by his sibling Set, who desired the lofty position. Osiris' passing prompted a power vacuum, and the divine beings mediated, requiring a court to choose the legitimate successor. The court, comprising of the lords of the Ennead, decided for Horus, announcing him the legitimate ruler.
The contention among Horus and Set is a common subject in Egyptian folklore. In certain adaptations, the fights are epic, with Horus and Set changing into different creatures to acquire a benefit. In others, the divine beings go about as go betweens, endeavoring to accommodate the two competitors.

In spite of the varieties in the fantasy, a definitive victory of Horus over Set represents the triumph of request and legitimate sovereignty over confusion.

Emblematic Implications and Characteristics:
Horus epitomizes a large number of representative implications, mirroring the different parts of Egyptian strict and social convictions. A few critical traits and affiliations include:

Majesty and Heavenly Power: As the child of Osiris, Horus was viewed as the genuine beneficiary of the privileged position of Egypt. The pharaohs distinguished themselves with Horus, supporting their heavenly right to run the show. The "Horus name" was one of the imperial titles expected by pharaohs.

Sky and Sun powered Imagery: Horus' relationship with the sky and the sun accentuated his heavenly nature. He was frequently connected to the sun god Ra, representing the sun's excursion across the sky every day. The hawk, with its capacity to take off high overhead, reflected the sun's direction.

Defensive Divinity: The Eye of Horus, a strong defensive image, was accepted to bring wellbeing and avert evil. It was many times utilized in special necklaces and other defensive charms. The Eye of Horus was additionally connected with the lunar cycles, underscoring the interconnectedness of the sun and the moon.

Image of Watchfulness and Equity: The hawk's sharp visual perception made it an image of carefulness and equity. Horus, with his sharp vision, was viewed as a careful watchman who could recognize and overcome any powers of confusion that compromised the heavenly request.

Factions and Sanctuaries Devoted to Horus:
The love of Horus was far reaching all through antiquated Egypt, and various sanctuaries were devoted to him the nation over. One of the most renowned is the Sanctuary of Horus at Edfu, situated on the west bank of the Nile. This sanctuary, worked during the Ptolemaic time frame (332-30 BCE), is surprisingly very much protected and gives significant experiences into the strict practices related with Horus. The religion of Horus stretched out past Edfu, with other significant focuses of love, including Behdet (cutting edge Damanhur) and Hierakonpolis. Every area had its own variation of the Horus legend and exceptional customs related with the god. Explorers and enthusiasts headed out to these sacrosanct destinations to look for the blessing and security of Horus.

Syncretism and Associations with Different Gods:
As Egyptian human advancement developed, so did the strict scene. One eminent viewpoint is the syncretism — the converging of various strict convictions and practices — bringing about the combination of divinities. Horus, as well, went through syncretic associations with different divine beings.
One such model is the combination of Horus with Ra, the strong sun god. The subsequent god, known as Ra-Horakhty, encapsulated the sun's excursion across the sky and the overall force of the sun powered circle. This syncretism built up the sun based parts of Horus' imagery and featured his association with the everyday pattern of the sun.

Heritage and Impact:
The love of Horus went on for centuries, persevering through the different periods of Egyptian history. Indeed, even after the downfall of old Egyptian progress, the folklore of Horus left an enduring effect on ensuing societies and conviction frameworks.
The idea of a heavenly figure with a bird of prey's head found reverberations in different legends, representing the getting through original imagery related with Horus. In the Greek period, the Greeks recognized Horus with their god Apollo, underlining the sun based and prophetic parts of the two divinities.
In current times, Horus stays a famous and conspicuous figure, frequently conjured in conversations of old Egyptian religion and folklore. His picture has tracked down a spot in mainstream society, showing up in workmanship, writing, and, surprisingly, motivating the naming of space apparatus and missions investigating the secrets of room.

2.2 Greek mythology: The messenger god Hermes and his winged sandals

Greek folklore is a mother lode of divine beings and goddesses, each with their own novel credits and jobs in the enormous request. Among the Olympian divinities, Hermes stands apart as the naughty and complex courier god, known for his mind, sly, and quickness. One of the most famous images related with Hermes is his winged shoes, a heavenly curio that epitomizes the god's job as a courier between the domains of divine beings and humans.

The Starting points of Hermes:
Hermes, the child of Zeus and the sprite Maia, was brought into the world in a cavern on Mount Cyllene in Paradise. His introduction to the world was covered in mystery, as Zeus tried to safeguard him from the anger of Hera, his better half. Notwithstanding his unassuming beginnings, Hermes immediately stood up for himself as a lord of extraordinary impact, assuming different parts inside the pantheon.

In the Homeric Psalm to Hermes, the god's finesse nature is apparent since the beginning. As a baby, he showed striking knowledge and creativity, qualities that would characterize his job as a middle person and courier in the heavenly order.

Characteristics and Images of Hermes:
Hermes is many times portrayed as a young and athletic figure, decorated with an explorer's cap, a winged staff known as the caduceus, and, obviously, the winged shoes. The caduceus, laced with two snakes, fills in as an image of business, heraldry, and strategy. It further underlines Hermes' job as a courier, communicator, and facilitator of tranquil dealings.
In any case, it is the winged shoes, known as "sandal," that catch the creative mind and interest of the people who dig into the stories of Greek folklore. These heavenly shoes, truly to Hermes by Zeus, enrich the god with the influence of flight and unmatched quickness.

The Making of the Winged Shoes:
The beginning of the winged shoes is established in the consequence of the Titanomachy, the legendary fight between the Titans and the Olympian divine beings for control of the universe. Following the triumph of the Olympians, Zeus looked to remunerate his heavenly posterity for their dependability and boldness. Among these prizes was the production of the winged shoes for Hermes.
Made by the heavenly smithies, the Cyclopes, and the lord of craftsmanship, Hephaestus, the winged shoes were a wonder of heavenly designing. The shoes were supposed to be produced using long-lasting gold and embellished with mind boggling feathers, furnishing Hermes with the capacity to navigate huge spans with amazing velocity. This striking footwear turned into a basic piece of Hermes' personality and assumed a urgent part in his different endeavors.

Hermes as the Courier of the Divine beings:
The essential job of Hermes was that of a courier, filling in as the mediator between the lords of Olympus and the human world. He was liable for conveying heavenly messages, orders, and pronouncements from the divine beings to humankind. This essential job situated Hermes as a scaffold between the heavenly and mortal domains, mirroring the interconnectedness of the grandiose request.
Hermes' quickness, worked with by the winged shoes, permitted him to go between Olympus, the domain of the divine beings, and the human world with unrivaled speed. This made him an irreplaceable figure in the unfurling of both heavenly and mortal undertakings. Notwithstanding his job as a courier, Hermes was likewise the aide of spirits to the Hidden world, accompanying the left to the domain of Abbadon.

Hermes in Fanciful Adventures:
The winged shoes assumed a vital part in large numbers of Hermes' fanciful endeavors, exhibiting both their commonsense utility and emblematic importance. One of the most notable stories including the winged shoes is the killing of the hundred-peered toward monster, Argus Panoptes.
Zeus had gone gaga for the fairy Io, and to shield her from the envious rage of Hera, he changed Io into a yearling. To oversee her, Hera relegated Argus Panoptes, a monster with 100 eyes, to watch Io. Resolute by the test, Hermes utilized his resourcefulness and the speed conceded by his winged shoes to hush Argus to lay down with a hypnotizing story. In a quick and thinking for even a second to move, Hermes then slew the goliath, freeing Io from her careful capturer.
The winged shoes were likewise instrumental in Hermes' job as a comedian and a cheat. In one occurrence, Hermes took Apollo's holy steers not long after his introduction to the world. To cover his tracks, he molded shoes out of myrtle branches to leave befuddling tracks that steered Apollo off course. This trying accomplishment exhibited both Hermes' cunning and the quickness given by his winged shoes.

Emblematic Implications of the Winged Shoes:
The winged shoes of Hermes convey profound emblematic implications that reach out past their commonsense use in working with quick travel. They encapsulate the ideas of speed, spryness, and the otherworldly idea of heavenly messages. The demonstration of flying with the winged shoes addresses the god's capacity to rise above natural limits and move easily between domains.
Besides, the winged shoes act as an image of Hermes' job as an aide and middle person. By empowering him to cross the domains of divine beings, humans, and the Hidden world, the shoes feature the god's diverse nature as a communicator, defender, and guide.

Social and Creative Portrayals:
The picture of Hermes with his winged shoes has penetrated different parts of Greek workmanship and culture. In traditional figure, container canvases, and other creative portrayals, Hermes is in many cases depicted in mid-flight, wings expanded, and shoes noticeably highlighted. These portrayals catch the dynamism and elegance related with the courier god.
The winged shoes have likewise enlivened later specialists and essayists, turning into an image of the greatness of human constraints. Their consideration in writing, compositions, and figures has kept on enamoring crowds, accentuating the persevering through allure of Greek folklore and its ageless subjects.

Heritage and Impact:
The tradition of Hermes, with his winged shoes, reaches out past the domain of Greek folklore. The idea of a quick courier with divine credits has tracked down reverberation in different societies and religions since the beginning of time. In Roman folklore, Hermes is compared with Mercury, the courier of the divine beings, accentuating the congruity of these model subjects across various social customs.
The imagery of quick couriers with winged footwear additionally shows up in Norse folklore with the figure of the god Loki, who has mystical shoes that empower him to rapidly travel immense distances. This equal mirrors the general interest with rising above impediments and accomplishing remarkable accomplishments.
In contemporary culture, the impact of Hermes and his winged shoes continues. The idea of a fast and productive courier is figuratively addressed in the cutting edge logo of the postal help, frequently highlighting a winged foot. Furthermore, the symbolism of winged shoes has advanced into mainstream society, showing up in writing, films, and different types of workmanship.

2.3   Hindu mythology: Garuda, the mount of Vishnu

In the tremendous and unpredictable embroidery of Hindu folklore, Garuda arises as an unmistakable and venerated figure, representing strength, unwaveringness, and heavenly help. As the mount of Ruler Vishnu, Garuda possesses a critical spot in the pantheon of Hindu gods, typifying both mythic glory and profound imagery. The story of Garuda unfurls inside the rich account of Hindu cosmology, offering experiences into the interchange between divine beings, devils, and the timeless battle for inestimable request.

The Starting points of Garuda:
Garuda's story starts with the early stage stirring of the sea, known as the Samudra Manthan, a grandiose occasion including divine beings and evil spirits taking a stab at the remedy of eternality, Amrita. As the beating strengthened, different heavenly creatures and fortunes rose up out of the sea profundities. Among these fortunes was Garuda, brought into the world from the egg that emerged during the stirring.
Garuda's introduction to the world is a demonstration of his heavenly parentage. His mom, Vinata, was one of the spouses of Kashyapa, an incredible sage, and his dad was the savvy's child, Aruna. Garuda, subsequently, acquired his mom's bird-like structure and his dad's brilliance, bringing about a glorious and impressive animal.

Garuda's Unwaveringness and Commitment:
Garuda's importance in Hindu folklore isn't exclusively founded on his impressive appearance; it is similarly grounded in his steady reliability and dedication to Master Vishnu.

As per the Puranas, Garuda was at first subjugated by the Nagas (snake creatures) because of a settlement between his mom Vinata and Kadru, the mother of the Nagas. To get the arrival of his mom, Garuda set out on a journey to get the Amrita, the nectar of everlasting status.

Mindful of Garuda's main goal, the divine beings mediated, offering him the Amrita in return for his loyalty. Nonetheless, Garuda's dedication to Vishnu beat his longing for eternality. In a demonstration of magnanimity, he decided to put the Amrita in the possession of the divine beings and turned into the everlasting mount of Master Vishnu. This sacrificial demonstration of penance and faithfulness charmed Garuda to Vishnu, laying out a profound and getting through connection between them.

Garuda and Master Vishnu:

Garuda's job as the mount of Master Vishnu isn't only emblematic; it means the indivisible association between the heavenly and the supernatural. In Hindu iconography, Ruler Vishnu is in many cases portrayed riding on the rear of Garuda, stressing the god's authority over the enormous powers and his dependence on the falcon like animal for quick and unhampered travel.

The harmonious connection among Vishnu and Garuda is exhibited in different Hindu sacred writings, including the Puranas and the stories Ramayana and Mahabharata. In the Ramayana, Garuda assumes a urgent part in the salvage of Sita, the associate of Ruler Rama, from the devil lord Ravana. His intercession works with the excursion of Rama and his partners to Lanka, highlighting Garuda's job as a facilitator of heavenly missions.

Garuda in Hindu Cosmology:

In the more extensive setting of Hindu cosmology, Garuda's importance reaches out past being a simple mount. He is viewed as the ruler of birds, addressing the zenith of avian strength and magnificence. Furthermore, Garuda is related with the idea of Prana, the existence force or crucial energy that penetrates the universe. In this perspective, he represents the grandiose breath and the interconnectedness of every living being. Garuda's presence in Hindu cosmology likewise lines up with the idea of dharma, or honest obligation. His relentless obligation to satisfying his mom's commitment and his ensuing faithfulness to Master Vishnu represent the adherence to one's dharma, even notwithstanding difficulty.

Imagery of Garuda:

Garuda epitomizes a huge number of emblematic implications inside Hindu folklore, mirroring the intricacy and profundity of the strict and philosophical practices. A few key representative credits related with Garuda include:

Strength and Power: Garuda's glorious and strong structure represents the strength that rises above the actual domain. As the lord of birds, he addresses the apex of avian ability and flexibility.

Commitment and Steadfastness: Garuda's benevolent dedication to Ruler Vishnu embodies the most elevated type of bhakti (commitment) in Hinduism. His decision to focus on his obligation over private longings fills in as an immortal illustration of dependability and penance.

Amazing quality and Opportunity: In Hindu cosmology, Garuda is frequently connected with the idea of moksha, or freedom. His capacity to take off through the skies addresses the spirit's excursion towards amazing quality and extreme independence from the pattern of birth and demise.

Interconnectedness and Amicability: Garuda's job as the transporter of Master Vishnu implies the agreeable harmony between various powers known to man. The organization among divine beings and their mounts highlights the interconnectedness and reliance of different heavenly substances in keeping vast control.

Garuda in Workmanship and Love:
The symbolism of Garuda is a repetitive theme in Hindu craftsmanship, figure, and sanctuary design. Portrayals of Garuda embellish numerous sanctuaries devoted to Ruler Vishnu, underlining the indivisible connection between the heavenly team. In these portrayals, Garuda is frequently depicted with outstretched wings, a bill, and claws, catching the pith of his glorious and magnificent nature.
Garuda is likewise loved autonomously in Hinduism. Sanctuaries committed exclusively to Garuda can be found across India, where aficionados offer petitions and perform customs to look for his favors for insurance and liberation from deterrents. The Garuda Purana, one of the eighteen Mahapuranas, is committed to the lessons and folklore related with Garuda.

Garuda and Then some:
While Garuda holds a focal spot in Hindu folklore, his impact reaches out past the limits of this strict practice. The idea of a heavenly bird, representing strength, dedication, and greatness, resounds with different societies and conviction frameworks around the world.
In Southeast Asian societies, especially in Indonesia and Thailand, Garuda is a public image and shows up on public seals, banners, and different social curios.

The personality of Garuda has likewise tracked down its direction into contemporary writing, craftsmanship, and mainstream society, vouching for the persevering through allure and pertinence of this legendary animal.

Chapter 3
Birds of the Sky and Creation

Birds, with their effortless flight and pleasant melodies, have caught the human creative mind over the entire course of time. Across societies and civilizations, birds play played critical parts in fantasies, creation stories, and emblematic portrayals. This investigation dives into the multi-layered associations between birds of the sky and the idea of creation, looking at how these avian animals have woven themselves into the rich embroidered artwork of human convictions, fables, and social articulations.

1. Birds in Creation Fantasies:
1.1. Phoenix: The Image of Resurrection:
Perhaps of the most famous bird in creation fantasies is the Phoenix. Across different societies, from old Egypt to China and Greece, the Phoenix is an image of restoration, revival, and the repetitive idea of life. As per the legend, the Phoenix consumes itself on fire upon death, just to rise again from its remains. This everlasting cycle turned into a strong similitude for creation, obliteration, and the constant recovery of the universe.

1.2. Garuda in Hindu Folklore:
In Hindu folklore, the Garuda, a legendary bird and the mount of Ruler Vishnu, assumes a significant part in creation stories. Garuda represents the victory of goodness over bad habit, encapsulating the vast request. His flight addresses the otherworldly excursion of the spirit, and his job as Vishnu's mount highlights the interconnectedness of vast powers in keeping up with equilibrium and request.

1.3. Alkonost and Sirin in Russian Old stories:
Russian old stories presents the Alkonost and Sirin, two legendary birds related with creation and the hereafter. The Alkonost's tune is supposed to be captivating to the point that it gives pleasure and serenity, while the Sirin's melody predicts a heavenly misfortune. These birds, with their magical tunes, span the domains of the living and the dead, forming the account of creation and fate in Russian folklore.

1.4. The Chicken in Chinese Folklore:
In Chinese folklore, the Red Chicken is a heavenly animal that crowed toward the start of creation, flagging the rise of light and the partition of yin and yang. The crowing of the chicken is accepted to disperse dimness and deliver the day break, making it an image of creation, arousing, and the repeating idea of time.

2. Birds as Couriers and Arbiters:

2.1. The Pigeon in Abrahamic Religions:

The pigeon is a common image in Abrahamic religions, addressing harmony, virtue, and heavenly correspondence. In the scriptural story of Noah's Ark, a pigeon is sent by Noah to track down dry land, representing trust, recharging, and the foundation of another pledge among God and humankind. In Christianity, the Essence of God is much of the time represented by a pigeon, further featuring the bird's job as a courier of heavenly will.

2.2. The Courier Crow in Local American Folklore:

In Local American folklore, the crow is much of the time depicted as a courier between the natural domain and the soul world. Crows are thought of as exceptionally canny and are accepted to have profound bits of knowledge. Their presence is viewed as a middle person among people and the heavenly, stressing their part in the otherworldly texture of creation.

2.3. The Owl in Greek Folklore:

In Greek folklore, the owl is related with Athena, the goddess of shrewdness. The owl's nighttime nature and its capacity to find in obscurity represent instinctive information and prescience. As a friend of Athena, the owl fills in as a middle person between the human and heavenly domains, encapsulating the association among shrewdness and creation.

2.4. The Quetzal in Mayan Culture:

The quetzal, an energetically hued bird local to Focal America, holds significant importance in Mayan folklore. Venerated as the "Dazzling Quetzal," this bird is related with the god Quetzalcoatl, a maker god. The quetzal's brilliant plumage and tricky nature represent the heavenly magnificence and secret intrinsic in the demonstration of creation.

3. Birds as Images of Change and Change:

3.1. The Swan in Hindu and Celtic Customs:

In Hindu folklore, the swan, or "hamsa," addresses the spirit's excursion towards self-acknowledgment and illumination. The swan is said to have the capacity to isolate milk from water, representing acumen between the fleeting and the timeless. Essentially, in Celtic folklore, swans are related with change and amazing quality, frequently portrayed as creatures fit for moving between the natural and Otherworld domains.

3.2. The Peacock in Hindu and Greco-Roman Folklore:

The peacock, with its dynamic plumage, holds assorted imagery in various societies. In Hindu folklore, the peacock is related with Saraswati, the goddess of astuteness and expressions. In Greco-Roman folklore, the peacock is connected to Hera and Juno, addressing everlasting status and the omnipresent eyes on the plumes representing heavenly information.

3.3. The Thunderbird in Local American Folklore:

In Local American folklore, the Thunderbird is a strong and grand animal related with rainstorms and change. Frequently depicted with wings spread wide, the Thunderbird represents the harmony between normal powers and the extraordinary force of tempests, adding to the patterns of creation and recharging in nature.

3.4. The Simurgh in Persian Folklore:

The Simurgh, a legendary bird in Persian writing, is an image of refinement and profound change. In the legendary sonnet "Gathering of the Birds" by Attar of Nishapur, the Simurgh is the final location of the birds on their otherworldly journey. This metaphorical story investigates the topic of self-revelation and the groundbreaking excursion of the spirit.

4. Birds in Social Imagery:

4.1. The Crane in Japanese Culture:

In Japanese old stories and workmanship, the crane is loved as an image of life span, satisfaction, and loyalty. The "Tsuru" (crane) is much of the time portrayed in customary origami, where collapsing 1,000 cranes is accepted to concede a wish. The crane's elegant flight and monogamous nature add to its portrayal of persevering through adoration and the immortal parts of creation.

4.2. The Raven in Norse Folklore:

In Norse folklore, the raven is related with Odin, the All-Father. Huginn and Muninn, Odin's two ravens, address thought and memory, separately. These ravens navigate the world every day, gathering data and taking it back to Odin. The raven's knowledge and job as couriers highlight its importance in the Norse enormous request.

4.3. The Kiwi in Maori Culture:

In Maori folklore, the kiwi bird is an image of uniqueness, singularity, and association with the land. The kiwi's nighttime propensities and its bashful, subtle nature add to its portrayal of otherworldly importance and the characteristic connection between individuals and the regular world in Maori cosmology.

4.4. The Hummingbird in Local American and South American Societies:

In Local American societies, especially in the Pueblo custom, the hummingbird represents love, excellence, and the capacity to give pleasure to other people. In South American societies, particularly in Aztec folklore, the hummingbird addresses revival and the transient idea of life. Its dynamic tones and spry flight add to its emblematic association with creation and the pattern of life.

5. Birds in Customs and Services:
5.1. Falconry in Islamic Practice:
Falconry, the craft of preparing and involving birds of prey for hunting, holds social importance in Islamic custom. Birds of prey, particularly the Peregrine Hawk, are exceptionally respected in Middle Easterner societies. The imagery of the hawk reaches out past hunting to address honorability, power, and accuracy, mirroring the cozy connection among people and birds in Islamic history.

5.2. The Owl in Local American Customs:
In Local American customs, the owl is frequently connected with astuteness, instinct, and premonition. The unmistakable calls of owls are accepted to pass on messages from the soul world. A few Local American clans perform owl moves, regarding the bird's association with profound direction and the inconspicuous domains.

5.3. The Chicken in Chinese New Year Festivities:
In Chinese culture, the chicken is an unmistakable image of favorable luck and constancy. During Chinese New Year festivities, the crowing of a chicken is accepted to bring gifts and avert fiendish spirits. The chicken's job in proclaiming the sunrise likewise represents the commitment of a fresh start and the recurrent idea of time.

3.1   Norse mythology: The role of ravens in Odin's wisdom
Norse folklore, with its mind boggling stories of divine beings, monsters, and powerful domains, is a mother lode of imagery and insight. Among the numerous divinities in the Norse pantheon, Odin, the All-Father, remains as a focal figure related with shrewdness, sorcery, and war. Ravens, especially Huginn and Muninn, his two confided in mates, assume a significant part in the enormous request and Odin's mission for information. This investigation digs into the meaning of ravens in Norse folklore, disentangling the layers of imagery, mythic stories, and social repeats that encompass these mysterious birds.

Odin, the All-Father:

To fathom the job of ravens in Norse folklore, one must initially dive into the personality of Odin. As the head of the Aesir, the chief gathering of divinities in Norse folklore, Odin reigns from his lofty position in Asgard, the domain of the divine beings. Known by many titles — All-Father, Drifter, and Raven God — Odin exemplifies a perplexing exchange of intelligence, information, and the tenacious quest for grandiose insights.

Odin's unquenchable hunger for information drove him to forfeit one of his eyes at the Well of Mimir, a wellspring of significant insight. This act underlines the profundity of Odin's obligation to unwinding the secrets of the universe and acquiring bits of knowledge that would shape the destiny of divine beings and humans the same.

Huginn and Muninn: The Ravens of Thought and Memory:
Next to Odin are two ravens, Huginn and Muninn, whose names mean "Thought" and "Memory" in Old Norse. These ravens act as augmentations of Odin's own awareness, exemplifying unmistakable features of his mission for insight.

1. Huginn (Thought):
Huginn addresses the scholarly and thoughtful part of Odin's temperament. The raven's job is likened to a steady stream of considerations, noticing and engrossing data from the world. Huginn's flights take him across the domains, looking over the occasions and events, gathering information that adds to's how Odin might interpret the universe.

2. Muninn (Memory):
Muninn, then again, exemplifies the archive of memory and the maintenance of information. The raven's processes include making a trip to far off domains and getting back to Odin with reports, working as a living document of encounters and experiences. Muninn's memorable's capacity and review data is critical to Odin's essential insight and direction.

Together, Huginn and Muninn structure a unique pair, giving Odin a far reaching and consistently extending consciousness of the world. Their recurrent flights represent the steady course of thought, reflection, and recognition that powers Odin's quest for shrewdness.

The Ravens as Couriers:
Past their jobs as Odin's avian augmentations, Huginn and Muninn act as couriers between the heavenly and mortal domains. Their flights are not restricted to Asgard but rather reach out to Midgard (the domain of people) and then some. The ravens go about as channels, passing on data among divine beings and people, stressing the interconnectedness of all creatures in the Norse cosmology.

The possibility of couriers or middle people between universes is a repetitive theme in numerous folklores, mirroring the faith in a vast request that requires correspondence and trade between various domains. In Norse folklore, Huginn and Muninn represent this idea, working with the progression of information and fate across the limits of the heavenly and the unremarkable.

Ravens and Front lines:
The relationship of ravens with war and fight adds one more layer to their importance in Norse folklore. Odin, as well as being a searcher of shrewdness, is likewise a lord of war and a supporter of champions. Ravens, as flesh birds, are attracted to front lines, where they devour the fallen. This association among ravens and the result of contention is a striking portrayal of the double idea of war — obliteration and restoration.

1. Odin's Presence on the War zone:
As per Norse folklore, Odin would frequently appear on war zones, joined by a crowd of Valkyries, champion ladies who picked the most daring of the tumbled to join the positions of the Einherjar, Odin's picked heroes in Valhalla. Ravens would be available, flying above as observers to the unfurling occasions. This symbolism builds up the possibility that Odin's insight is personally attached to the patterns of life and demise, where the ravens act as harbingers of both conflict and the inescapable change to the great beyond.

2. Ravens and Valkyries:
The association among ravens and Valkyries goes past simple perception. In certain understandings of Norse folklore, it is proposed that the Valkyries can shape-shift into ravens. This change permits them to move consistently between the human and heavenly domains, underlining the smoothness of presence and the interconnectedness of the profound and material universes.

Imagery of the Ravens:
The imagery encompassing Huginn and Muninn in Norse folklore is rich and layered, reflecting subjects of shrewdness, duality, and the recurrent idea of presence.

1. Astuteness and Information:
The ravens encapsulate the quest for intelligence through thought and memory. Huginn's job as "Thought" addresses the consistent scholarly movement, request, and examination expected for getting information. Muninn's job as "Memory" addresses the maintenance and review of previous encounters, bits of knowledge, and illustrations. Together, they structure an all encompassing way to deal with intelligence, mirroring Odin's far reaching comprehension of the world.

2. Duality and Equilibrium:

The matching of Huginn and Muninn additionally represents the fragile harmony among thought and memory, acumen and feeling, activity and reflection. Odin's insight emerges from the agreeable transaction of these dualities, underscoring the significance of equilibrium in one's quest for information and understanding.

3. Association with Destiny and Fate:

Ravens, as couriers and observers on war zones, are connected to the idea of destiny, known as "wyrd" in Old Norse. The ravens' presence highlights the certainty of predetermination and the interconnected strings that weave the embroidered artwork of presence. Their flights represent the consistent progression of situation and the developing of foreordained destinies.

4. Demise and Restoration:

The relationship of ravens with death, especially on war zones, lines up with the Norse confidence in recurrent life and demise. The devouring of ravens on the fallen isn't an image of grim interest but instead a portrayal of the normal request of life, where demise is entwined with the potential for resurrection and recharging.

5. Watchmen of the Runes:

In a few Norse customs, ravens are viewed as watchmen of the runes, old images pervaded with supernatural and enchanted importance. Runes are accepted to hold the way to opening secret insights and getting to the information implanted in the texture of the universe. The ravens' association with the runes supports their job as conductors of heavenly insight and supernatural bits of knowledge.

Social Reverberations and Present day Translations:

The imagery of ravens in Norse folklore has made a permanent imprint on social articulations, writing, and, surprisingly, current understandings of the past.

1. Scholarly Impacts:

Norse folklore, with its striking characters and many-sided accounts, has roused various works of writing. The ravens, as necessary parts of Odin's personality, frequently wind up woven into the embroidery of these accounts. From J.R.R. Tolkien's "The Hobbit" and "The Ruler of the Rings" to Neil Gaiman's "American Divine beings," the reverberations of Huginn and Muninn resound in the minds of contemporary perusers.

2. Mainstream society References:

Ravens, as images of shrewdness and secret, have become famous themes in contemporary mainstream society.

Whether in motion pictures, computer games, or realistic books, the confounding charm of ravens is frequently saddled to convey a feeling of old information, sorcery, and extraordinary insight.

3. Imaginative Portrayals:
The imaginative portrayals of Odin joined by his ravens are notorious in Norse workmanship. Canvases, figures, and representations frequently catch the magnificence of Odin with Huginn and Muninn roosted on his shoulders or in flight. These portrayals act as visual tokens of the profound social roots and representative extravagance implanted in Norse folklore.

4. Norse Restoration and Neo-Agnosticism:
The resurgence of interest in Norse folklore, some of the time alluded to as the Norse restoration, has prompted a recharged appreciation for the imagery of ravens. In neo-agnostic and Pagan people group, the ravens are worshipped as images of direction, shrewdness, and otherworldly association. The Norse pantheon, including Odin and his ravens, is embraced as a wellspring of motivation for contemporary profound practices.

3.2   Indigenous cultures: The Thunderbird and its significance
Native societies all over the planet are rich with significant imagery, legendary animals, and otherworldly accounts that typify their profound association with the normal world. Among these, the Thunderbird stands apart as a great and worshipped image, rising above local and ancestral differentiations. This investigation digs into the meaning of the Thunderbird in Native societies, disentangling its complex jobs as an image of force, otherworldliness, and the amicable exchange among humankind and the universe.

1. Starting points and Variety of Thunderbird Legend:
The Thunderbird is a legendary animal profoundly dug in the oral customs of different Native people groups across North America. While explicit subtleties and characteristics might shift among various clans, the Thunderbird for the most part possesses a focal spot in the aggregate folklore of these different societies.

1.1. Geographic Variety:
The Thunderbird is quite present in the legend of clans, for example, the Ojibwe, Ho-Piece, Algonquin, and Haida, among others. Regardless of the geographic variety of these clans, the Thunderbird's importance remains astoundingly steady, featuring its all inclusive allure and social reverberation.

1.2. Portrayals in Craftsmanship and Customs:

The Thunderbird is many times portrayed in native craftsmanship, including chain of commands, covers, and formal attire. Its symbolism reaches out past visual portrayals, tracking down articulation in tunes, moves, and customs that commend its power and otherworldly importance. The bird's unmistakable presence in these social articulations underlines its persevering through significance in the regular routines and services of Native people group.

2. Imagery of the Thunderbird:

The Thunderbird conveys an abundance of imagery that rises above its portrayal as a simple animal. Its importance reaches out into the domains of otherworldliness, power, and the regular powers that oversee the universe.

2.1. Power and Territory Over the Sky:

Fundamental to the Thunderbird's imagery is its relationship with the sky and the essential powers of lightning storm. In different Native conviction frameworks, the Thunderbird is viewed as a strong being with command over storms. The beating of its wings is said to deliver thunder, and the glimmering of its eyes makes lightning. This predominance over the sky connotes the animal's monstrous power and impact.

2.2. Gatekeeper Soul and Defender:

The Thunderbird is many times loved as a watchman soul and defender of individuals. In numerous Native societies, the bird is accepted to look after networks and people, offering both physical and profound security. Its presence is conjured in customs and functions to look for direction and gifts, mirroring the profound feeling of trust and adoration agreed to this legendary being.

2.3. Change and Shapeshifting:

In certain practices, the Thunderbird is related with the capacity to shapeshift, changing from bird to human structure. This groundbreaking perspective highlights the ease of profound domains and the interconnectedness of every single living being. The Thunderbird's capacity to navigate the limits between the avian and human universes represents a scaffold between the natural and the heavenly.

2.4. Image of Solidarity and Power:

The Thunderbird is likewise viewed as an image of solidarity and power among Native countries. Its portrayal in ancestral tokens and banners implies a common character and aggregate strength. The Thunderbird fills in as the need might have arisen to beat difficulties, cultivating a feeling of local area and social pride.

3. Thunderbird in Mythic Accounts:

The Thunderbird's importance is profoundly implanted in mythic accounts that explain its beginnings, activities, and communications with other legendary creatures.

3.1. Creation Stories:

In some Native creation stories, the Thunderbird assumes a critical part in the development of the world. It is many times depicted as an animal of incredible power whose activities add to the forming of scenes and the foundation of regular request. The Thunderbird's job as a main player in creation stories highlights its status as a basic power in the cosmogony of Native societies.

3.2. Courageous Adventures:

Mythic stories likewise portray the Thunderbird as a courageous figure participated in legendary clashes with other heavenly creatures, like the Incomparable Horned Snake. These accounts exhibit the Thunderbird's mental fortitude, strength, and assurance to keep up with balance in the profound and normal domains. The Thunderbird's endeavors become a wellspring of motivation for Native people group, imparting a feeling of flexibility and boldness despite misfortune.

3.3. Extraordinary Excursions:

A few stories feature the Thunderbird's extraordinary excursions between the physical and otherworldly universes. These excursions frequently include experiences with other legendary creatures or spirits, stressing the interconnectedness of the Thunderbird with the more extensive profound biological system. The bird's journeys become symbolic stories that convey examples of astuteness, flexibility, and the repeating idea of presence.

4. Thunderbird in Social Practices:

The Thunderbird's impact reaches out into different social works on, including functions, moves, and creative articulations that praise its emblematic reverberation.

4.1. Thunderbird Moves:

In numerous Native people group, Thunderbird moves are fundamental to stylized customs. These moves, joined by cadenced drumming and reciting, try to conjure the soul of the Thunderbird. Members frequently wear formal attire decorated with Thunderbird images, encapsulating the bird's solidarity and effortlessness in their developments. These moves act for of interfacing with the otherworldly domain and looking for the Thunderbird's endowments for the local area.

4.2. Thunderbird Craftsmanship:

Imaginative portrayals of the Thunderbird are common in native fine arts. From complicatedly cut chain of commands to lively works of art and beadwork, the Thunderbird's picture is a repetitive theme. These imaginative articulations not just grandstand the inventiveness and expertise of native craftsmen yet in addition act as visual tokens of the bird's social importance and otherworldly power.

4.3. Emblematic Enhancements:

Images of the Thunderbird frequently enhance customary formal attire, articles of clothing, and stately things. These images might incorporate portrayals of the Thunderbird's outstretched wings, sharp nose, and claws. The deliberate consideration of Thunderbird symbolism in social embellishments mirrors a craving to conjure the bird's defensive soul and bridle its representative power during significant services and transitional experiences.

5. Thunderbird in Contemporary Setting:

The Thunderbird's significance and reverberation endure in contemporary Native settings, where endeavors to save and renew social customs are continuous.

5.1. Social Restoration:

Despite authentic difficulties and social osmosis, numerous Native people group are effectively participated in social renewal endeavors. The Thunderbird, with its profound roots in fantasy, otherworldliness, and imagery, assumes a focal part in these drives. Social evangelist and specialists draw upon the Thunderbird's symbolism to reconnect with tribal customs and send social information to people in the future.

5.2. Ecological Support:

The Thunderbird's relationship with the normal components, especially the sky and tempests, lines up with contemporary Native points of view on natural stewardship. A few Native gatherings view the Thunderbird as an image of environmental equilibrium and supporter for preservation measures to safeguard the regular world, propelled by the bird's legendary association with the world's rhythms.

5.3. Instructive Drives:

Instructive projects inside Native people group frequently integrate Thunderbird imagery to bestow social lessons and values. The bird's credits, like strength, insurance, and solidarity, become instructive similitudes that reverberate with Native youth, cultivating a feeling of social pride and character.

3.3   Chinese mythology: The phoenix and its symbolism of rebirth

In the tremendous embroidery of Chinese folklore, the phoenix, known as Fenghuang (凤凰), remains as a lofty image of resurrection, recharging, and the repetitive idea of presence. Dissimilar to the Western idea of a phoenix coming back to life, the Chinese phoenix encapsulates an exceptional arrangement of social, profound, and vast meanings well established in old Chinese convictions. This investigation dives into the rich imagery of the phoenix in Chinese folklore, disentangling job as a legendary animal rises above time, epitomizing topics of change and everlasting restoration.

1. Legendary Beginnings of the Fenghuang:

The Fenghuang, frequently alluded to as the Chinese phoenix, is a legendary bird with beginnings going back millennia. Its presence in Chinese folklore is entwined with heavenly cosmologies, majestic iconography, and social stories that portray the bird as an image of favorability and heavenly effortlessness.

1.1. Dualities and Representative Pairings:

In Chinese folklore, the Fenghuang is frequently matched with the mythical beast, framing an emblematic duality known as Lengthy Feng Cheng Xiang (龙凤呈祥), where the winged serpent addresses the male rule (yang) and the phoenix represents the female standard (yin). This association implies amicability, balance, and the inestimable transaction between corresponding powers. The winged serpent and phoenix theme regularly shows up in customary Chinese craftsmanship, materials, and design components, epitomizing the agreeable equilibrium of restricting energies.

1.2. Feng and Huang:

The expression "Fenghuang" is a composite of two birds, the Feng (凤) and the Huang (凰). The Feng addresses the male phoenix, while the Huang addresses the female phoenix. In old Chinese cosmology, the Fenghuang is viewed as a particular animal enveloping both male and female qualities, supporting the idea of equilibrium and fulfillment.

2. Imagery of the Fenghuang:

The Fenghuang conveys a rich embroidery of imagery, each quill and quality adding to its diverse importance in Chinese folklore.

2.1. Resurrection and Eternality:
Integral to the imagery of the Fenghuang is the idea of resurrection and everlasting status. Dissimilar to the Western phoenix, which is related with repeating recovery through fire, the Chinese phoenix addresses an everlasting pattern of recharging without the damaging component of obliteration.
The Fenghuang's capacity to kick the bucket and be reawakened builds up the more extensive Chinese social confidence in the repetitive idea of life, passing, and restoration.

2.2. Image of Goodness and Beauty:
The Fenghuang is frequently connected with goodness, beauty, and consideration. In Chinese culture, it represents the presence of an ethical ruler or a period of tranquil administration. The bird's rich plumage, dazzling tones, and elegant disposition act as seals of moral greatness and agreeable initiative. The presence of the Fenghuang is viewed as a promising sign, proclaiming a period of flourishing and uprightness.

2.3. Enormous Imagery:
In Chinese cosmology, the Fenghuang is in some cases related with the five components — wood, fire, earth, metal, and water. The bird's lively plumage is said to address these components, stressing its association with the principal building blocks of the universe. The Fenghuang's presence is accepted to bring infinite equilibrium and arrangement, encouraging amicability between the divine and natural domains.

2.4. Reverberation with Yin and Yang:
As a legendary animal epitomizing both male and female characteristics, the Fenghuang lines up with the standards of yin and yang. Its duality reflects the correlative powers that underlie the astronomical request, underscoring the significance of equilibrium and balance. The Fenghuang's imagery reverberates with more extensive Taoist and Confucian ways of thinking, where concordance and equilibrium are regarded ethics.

3. Mythic Accounts Including the Fenghuang:
All through Chinese folklore, the Fenghuang shows up in different accounts and legends, adding to the social embroidered artwork of the divine bird.

3.1. The Fenghuang's Wedding:

One of the most notable fantasies including the Fenghuang is the narrative of its wedding, where the bird was said to pick a mate via arriving on the parts of a particular tree. This occasion was viewed as a favorable sign, connoting congruity and favorable luck. The Fenghuang's wedding turned into an image of positive starting points and the commitment of thriving.

3.2. Majestic Imagery:
In majestic settings, the Fenghuang held specific importance as an image of the sovereign and ruler partner.
The presence of the Fenghuang in magnificent iconography conveyed the possibility of an equitable and kind ruler. The bird embellished royal articles of clothing, furniture, and design, highlighting its relationship with the magnificent family and the thriving of the country.

3.3. Excursion toward the West:
In the exemplary Chinese scholarly work "Excursion toward the West," ascribed to the Ming administration creator Wu Cheng'en, the Fenghuang shows up. The bird is depicted as living in the Lobby of General Sound in the Western Heaven, featuring its divine and extraordinary nature. This portrayal further stresses the Fenghuang's association with divine domains and otherworldly real factors.

4. Social Portrayals and Creative Portrayals:
The Fenghuang's imagery stretches out into different parts of Chinese culture, including workmanship, writing, and day to day existence.

4.1. Craftsmanship and Enriching Expressions:
Creative portrayals of the Fenghuang are bountiful in conventional Chinese artistic expressions. Artworks, figures, and ceramics frequently portray the bird in grand quality, its plumage shining with energetic varieties. The Fenghuang's picture enhances materials, especially on wedding pieces of clothing, representing affection, constancy, and the commitment of an agreeable association.

4.2. Engineering and Plan:
The Fenghuang's impact is additionally apparent in building components. Sanctuaries, castles, and familial lobbies are embellished with carvings, reliefs, and works of art of the Fenghuang, instilling these designs with a feeling of holiness and heavenly security. The bird's picture is unpredictably woven into the texture of Chinese plan, mirroring its persevering through importance in molding social style.

4.3. Celebrations and Services:

The imagery of the Fenghuang is much of the time conjured during happy events and services. Festivities like weddings, New Year's celebrations, and significant widespread developments might integrate the bird's symbolism as a harbinger of bliss, flourishing, and positive starting points. The Fenghuang's presence in these settings supports its job as an image of propitiousness and heavenly blessing.

5. Fenghuang in Contemporary Culture:

In contemporary China, the imagery of the Fenghuang keeps on being pertinent, adjusting to present day settings while holding its profound social roots.

5.1. Present day Craftsmanship and Plan:

Contemporary specialists frequently attract upon the Fenghuang's imagery their works, mixing conventional themes with current style. The bird's picture is highlighted in style, adornments, and inside plan, associating contemporary crowds with antiquated social stories.

5.2. Social Recovery and Mindfulness:

As China goes through fast friendly and social changes, there is a restored interest in conventional legends and folklore. The Fenghuang, with its immortal imagery, turns into a point of convergence for social recovery and mindfulness. Endeavors to protect and celebrate conventional expressions, specialties, and stories guarantee that the Fenghuang's heritage perseveres in the hearts and brains of new ages.

5.3. Global Acknowledgment:

The Fenghuang's imagery has risen above public lines, catching the interest of individuals around the world. Its picture is at times highlighted in worldwide craftsmanship presentations, comprehensive developments, and cooperative tasks, filling in as a scaffold between Chinese folklore and worldwide crowds.

Chapter 4
Guardian Spirits and Animal Totems

In the huge embroidered artwork of human otherworldliness, the idea of gatekeeper spirits and creature emblems has woven itself into the texture of different societies across the globe. From the antiquated acts of native networks to the advanced translations inside contemporary otherworldly developments, the imagery and meaning of these profound aides persevere. This investigation dives into the rich and nuanced universe of watchman spirits and creature symbols, looking at their authentic roots, social varieties, and the persevering through pertinence they hold in forming human associations with the profound domain.

1. Presentation: Watchmen of the Soul, Attendants of Insight
1.1. Characterizing Watchman Spirits and Creature Symbols:
Watchman spirits and creature symbols are signs of otherworldly creatures or creatures that are accepted to offer direction, assurance, and knowledge to people or networks. Established in old animistic convictions, these ideas rise above topographical and social limits, mirroring a widespread human craving for association with the profound and regular universes.

1.2. Authentic Roots: Animism and Then some:
The starting points of gatekeeper spirits and creature symbols can be followed to animism, the conviction that all substances, including creatures, plants, and normal components, have an otherworldly pith. As humankind's earliest otherworldly system, animism established the groundwork for the comprehension that creatures could act as mediators between the commonplace and the heavenly.

1.3. Social Varieties: Across Mainlands and Customs:
While the major idea of watchman spirits and creature emblems is widespread, the particular creatures picked and their representative implications shift across societies. From the command hierarchies of Local American clans to the hereditary love in African social orders, each social setting saturates these otherworldly substances with remarkable importance, mirroring the different scenes and environments that shape human encounters.

2. Gatekeeper Spirits in Native Societies: Sustaining the Otherworldly Association
2.1. Local American Totemism: An Ensemble of Images:
In Local American societies, totemism is profoundly imbued, with command hierarchies filling in as fantastic articulations of otherworldly convictions. Creature emblems, going from bears to hawks, are venerated as gatekeeper spirits that aide, secure, and bestow insight to people and families. Every emblem creature conveys a particular imagery, addressing characteristics and illustrations that reverberate with the shared perspective of the local area.

2.2. African Genealogical Spirits: Watchmen of Genealogy:
In numerous African social orders, genealogical spirits, frequently addressed by creature symbols, assume a crucial part in directing and safeguarding the living. These watchman spirits are accepted to epitomize the insight and encounters of predecessors, offering an otherworldly connection among over a wide span of time. The worship for explicit creatures changes across districts, mirroring the assorted fauna that coincides with human networks.

2.3. Cold Shamanism: Creature Partners in the Frosty Wild:
Cold native societies, for example, the Inuit and Sami individuals, have a rich practice of shamanism where creature spirits are seen as strong partners. Shamans, in their profound excursions, look for direction and help from gatekeeper spirits encapsulated by creatures like the polar bear, reindeer, or wolf. The cruel Cold climate has encouraged a profound cooperative connection among people and the collective of animals, reflected in the otherworldly acts of these networks.

3. Creature Emblems in Asian Profound Customs: Images of Agreement and Equilibrium
3.1. Chinese Zodiac: Heavenly Creatures and Characters:
The Chinese zodiac, established in antiquated Chinese cosmology, relegates every year to one of twelve creatures, each conveying explicit characteristics and characteristics. These creatures act as something beyond images of time; they are accepted to impact the characters and predeterminations of people brought into the world under their impact. From the innovative Rodent to the lofty Mythical beast, the Chinese zodiac exhibits the significant association among creatures and human destiny.

3.2. Shinto and Japanese Creature Spirits: Kami in Nature:
In Shinto, the native otherworldliness of Japan, the faith in kami — profound substances dwelling in regular components — is profoundly imbued.

Numerous kami are related with creatures, mirroring the veneration for the regular world. Creatures like the fox and the deer are viewed as hallowed couriers and are frequently portrayed as watchman spirits in Shinto sanctuaries.

3.3. Hinduism and the Untouchable relic: An Image of Godliness:
In Hinduism, the cow holds a focal spot as a respected creature. Considered sacrosanct and an image of peacefulness, the cow is in excess of a watchman soul — it is a wellspring of sustenance, an image of overflow, and a portrayal of heavenly characteristics. The significant association among people and cows in Hindu culture stretches out past the material domain, underlining the profound meaning of this delicate animal.

4. Creature Emblems in African and Native Otherworldliness: Roots in Nature, Astuteness in Images
4.1. African Creature Emblems: Ancestral Insight and Emblematic Affiliations:
Across the different scenes of Africa, ancestral networks have created one of a kind associations with explicit creatures, seeing them as tribal images. The Baobab tree, the Elephant, or the Panther might act as emblems addressing ancestral personalities, otherworldly security, and the transmission of genealogical insight. These symbols are worshipped as gatekeepers, typifying the pith of the normal world.

4.2. Australian Native Dreamtime: Tribal Spirits in the Scene:
In Australian Native otherworldliness, the Dreamtime is a primary idea that envelops the production of the world and the continuous profound association between people, creatures, and the land. Tribal creatures, known as Dreaming precursors, are accepted to have molded the scene and proceed to direct and safeguard Native people group. These tribal spirits act as a living association with the Dreamtime, supporting the interconnectedness of all life.

5. Current Translations: Creature Emblems in Contemporary Otherworldliness
5.1. New Age Otherworldliness: Power Creatures and Self-awareness:
In contemporary otherworldly developments, especially inside the New Age development, the idea of force creatures has acquired fame. People try to interface with explicit creatures that impact them on a profound level, frequently in quest for self-improvement, direction, and recuperating. This advanced reevaluation draws motivation from native convictions while adjusting to the individualistic and varied nature of contemporary otherworldliness.

5.2. Totemism in Eco-Otherworldliness: Sustaining Earth Associations:
As natural mindfulness develops, a few people and networks have gone to totemism as
a type of eco-otherworldliness. Tribal images of creatures and normal components
become profound aides as well as tokens of mankind's interconnectedness with the
Earth. This advanced transformation of tribal practices highlights the significance of
ecological stewardship and respect for the regular world.

**5.3. Hallucinogenic Investigation and Creature Spirits: Shamanic Excursions of
the Brain:**
In the domain of hallucinogenic encounters and entheogenic functions, people
frequently report experiences with creature spirits or tribal elements. These
experiences, whether experienced through changed conditions of cognizance or
visionary excursions, equal shamanic customs where creatures act as advisers for
domains past customary insight. The imagery of these experiences frequently conveys
individual and aggregate importance.

6. Mental Points of view: Models, Images, and Inward Direction
6.1. Jungian Originals: Creature Emblems as Images of the Mind:
According to a mental point of view, the idea of creature emblems lines up with Carl
Jung's hypothesis of models — general images implanted in the aggregate oblivious.
Creatures, as original images, address parts of the human mind and act as advisers for
self-revelation. Investigating one's association with explicit creatures can give bits of
knowledge into the person's internal world and mental elements.

6.2. Inward Direction and Instinct: Creature Symbols as Otherworldly Partners:
For some people, the idea of creature symbols is a wellspring of inward direction and
instinct. Whether through reflection, dreams, or unconstrained experiences with explicit
creatures, individuals frequently feel a significant association with these creatures. This
natural association is viewed as a type of otherworldly direction, offering bits of
knowledge into individual difficulties, decisions, and valuable open doors for
development.

4.1 Native American traditions: The spiritual significance of eagles and owls

Local American practices are saturated with a significant association with the normal
world, where creatures are viewed as actual creatures as well as otherworldly elements
with novel characteristics and imagery. Among these loved animals, the hawk and the
owl hold extraordinary importance in different native societies across North America.

This investigation dives into the otherworldly significance of hawks and owls in Local American customs, unwinding the rich embroidered artwork of imagery, social practices, and the significant association between these birds and the profound domain.

1. The Hawk: Image of Force, Otherworldliness, and Opportunity
1.1. The Hawk in Local American Cosmology:
The hawk remains as an unmistakable figure in Local American cosmology, representing power, otherworldliness, and opportunity. Venerated for its sharp vision, magnificent flight, and association with the sky, the falcon is many times viewed as a courier between the natural and profound domains. Its presence overhead is viewed as an extension to the Maker, making it an image of heavenly correspondence.

1.2. Imagery of the Falcon Plume: A Sacrosanct Gift:
Among Local American clans, the falcon feather holds specific importance and is viewed as a hallowed gift from the bird. The plumes are utilized in different functions, ceremonies, and formal attire, implying honor, courage, and a profound association with the otherworldly world. The introduction of a falcon feather is a significant motion, representing appreciation, trust, and affirmation of a singular's accomplishments or commitments to the local area.

1.3. Ancestral Varieties: Falcons in Various Societies:
While the bird is worshipped across numerous Local American societies, there are varieties in its imagery and importance. For instance, among the Lakota Sioux, the bird is related with the Thunder Being, a strong and generous power in their cosmology. In Hopi customs, the hawk is a gatekeeper of the upper world and is many times conjured in ceremonies for downpour and horticultural overflow.

1.4. Bird Dance: Ceremonies of Recharging:
The Bird Dance is a stately dance drilled by a few Local American clans, including the Hopi and Zuni. This dance is a type of supplication and a custom of restoration, representing the association between the artists and the soul of the bird. The artists wear falcon plumes and epitomize the grand developments of the bird, conjuring the hawk's characteristics of solidarity, vision, and otherworldly understanding.

1.5. The Bald Eagle: Public Image and Profound Symbol:
The bald eagle, with its unmistakable white head and tail, holds a unique spot as a public image of the US. In any case, its importance goes past devoted symbols; the bald eagle is likewise an otherworldly symbol in Local American customs. Its taking off flight is viewed as an image of profound rising and a sign of the interconnectedness of every single living being.

2. The Owl: Courier of Insight and Secret
2.1. The Owl in Local American Old stories: An Image of Shrewdness:
The owl, with its nighttime propensities and perplexing presence, is viewed as a courier of shrewdness in Local American legends. Its capacity to explore the obscurity and see what others can't makes it an image of sharp understanding, instinct, and the capacity to see past the surface. The owl's secretive nature adjusts it to the soul world and the concealed domains.

2.2. Owl as an Aide in Dreamtime: Otherworldly Importance:
In a few Local American societies, the owl is accepted to be an aide in dreamtime, giving otherworldly bits of knowledge and messages to the people who experience it in their fantasies. The owl's appearance is many times seen as a sign that one ought to focus on their inward insight and natural resources. Dream experiences with owls are viewed as significant otherworldly encounters.

2.3. Ancestral Varieties: Owls Across Societies:
Various clans quality shifted imagery to the owl. For the Hopi public, the Tunneling Owl is related with horticultural ripeness and security. Among the Zuni, the owl is connected to the moon and its cycles, while the Ojibwe consider the owl to be a harbinger of death and an aide for the spirits of the departed. The variety of owl imagery mirrors the nuanced comprehension of these birds inside unmistakable social settings.

2.4. Owl Quills in Formal Use: Association with the Soul World:
Owl feathers are likewise used in Local American services, despite the fact that their utilization and imagery can shift among clans. The plumes might be integrated into ceremonial devices, formal attire, or holy items, connoting the owl's association with the soul world and its job as an aide in issues of the spirit.

2.5. Night Moves and Owl Ceremonies: Communing with the Soul Domain:
In certain clans, night moves and owl ceremonies are performed to conjure the soul of the owl. These functions are in many cases led under the front of haziness, upgrading the association between the members and the secretive domain represented by the owl. The customs are viewed for the purpose of looking for direction, security, and profound fellowship with the inconspicuous powers.

3. Stories and Legends: Accounts of Birds and Owls
3.1. Bird and Owl in Creation Stories:
Numerous Local American clans have creation stories that highlight the falcon and the owl as focal characters.

These accounts make sense of the starting points of the world, the connections among creatures and people, and the jobs played by these famous birds in forming the universe. Such accounts are gone down through ages, conveying the insight and social character of every clan.

3.2. The Owl Lady: Manager of Shrewdness and Reap:
In Hopi folklore, there is a worshipped figure known as the Owl Lady. She is viewed as a manager of shrewdness and the watchman of the gather. The Owl Lady is related with horticultural ripeness and is many times conjured in customs to guarantee a plentiful gather. Her presence connotes the nearby interconnection between nature, otherworldliness, and the prosperity of the local area.

3.3. Falcon and Thunderbird: Gatekeepers of the Skies:
In different Local American customs, the hawk is frequently connected with the Thunderbird, a strong and legendary animal associated with lightning storm. The Thunderbird is an image of heavenly power and is in some cases considered a divinity related with storms. The hawk's capacity to take off high overhead adjusts it to the Thunderbird's domain over the sky.

4. The Preservation Challenge: Safeguarding Consecrated Creatures
4.1. Legitimate Securities for Hawks: Adjusting Otherworldliness and Protection:
The profound meaning of hawks has presented difficulties with regards to natural life protection. While hawks are safeguarded under different regulations, including the Bare and Brilliant Falcon Assurance Act, Local American clans are allowed unique authorizations to utilize bird plumes and parts in their strict practices. This fragile harmony between social customs and preservation endeavors features the requirement for cooperative methodologies that regard both environmental respectability and otherworldly importance.

4.2. Dangers to Owl Populaces: Preservation Concerns:
Owls, as well, face preservation challenges because of natural surroundings misfortune, environmental change, and other ecological dangers. The profound meaning of owls in Local American societies adds an extra layer of worry for their prosperity. Endeavors to save owl populaces should think about the significance of these birds in social practices and guarantee that preservation measures are embraced with aversion to native points of view.

4.2 African mythology: The role of birds as protectors and guides

African folklore is a rich embroidery of different convictions, customs, and stories that mirror the landmass' social variety. Among the bunch images and substances inside African fanciful practices, birds hold a unique spot as defenders and guides. Across different societies and districts, birds are instilled with profound importance, exemplifying characteristics of shrewdness, assurance, and heavenly correspondence. This investigation digs into the complex job of birds in African folklore, unwinding the emblematic strings that associate these winged creatures to the profound domains of the mainland.

1. Avian Imagery in African Folklore:
1.1. Birds as Couriers of the Heavenly:
In African folklore, birds are frequently viewed as couriers of the heavenly, conveying messages between the natural and profound domains. Their capacity to cross the skies is representative of an association with the sky, making them conductors for correspondence with the divine beings and precursors. The presence of specific birds in unambiguous settings is accepted to convey significant profound messages and direction.

1.2. Consecrated Birds: Images of Shrewdness and Assurance:
Certain bird species are viewed as consecrated in African folklore, addressing shrewdness, security, and otherworldly knowledge. The imagery related with these birds shifts across societies, however normal subjects incorporate the exemplification of tribal insight, the vigilant guardianship of networks, and the capacity to direct people on their profound excursions.

1.3. Birds in Creation Legends: Developers of Universes:
In numerous African creation legends, birds assume an essential part as dynamic members in the molding of the world. A few fantasies portray birds as designers who help with building the universe, while others property the production of explicit components, like waterways or mountains, to the activities of heavenly avian creatures. These accounts highlight the fundamental job of birds in the primary accounts of African cosmogony.

2. The Hornbill: Image of Inestimable Agreement and Assurance:
2.1. The Southern Ground Hornbill: Precursor's Voice:
The Southern Ground Hornbill, known for its unmistakable appearance and profound, full calls, is adored in different African societies. In certain practices, the hornbill is accepted to convey the voice of the progenitors, settling on its decisions a type of genealogical correspondence.

The bird's presence is viewed as a defender of family and local area, underlining the significance of familial bonds and otherworldly congruity.

2.2. Yoruba Folklore: The Hornbill as Courier of Olokun:
In Yoruba folklore, the hornbill is related with Olokun, the Orisha of the ocean and abundance. The bird is viewed as a courier of Olokun and is accepted to carry messages from the god to the human domain. The hornbill's relationship with Olokun highlights its job as a conductor between the heavenly and human circles, typifying the interconnectedness of otherworldly and material parts of life.

2.3. Baule Individuals: The Hornbill and Eternity:
Among the Baule nation of Ivory Coast, the hornbill is connected to convictions about eternity. It is trusted that when an individual kicks the bucket, their spirit changes into a hornbill. The bird is viewed as an aide for the departed, assisting them with exploring the profound domains. This relationship with the excursion to eternity upgrades the hornbill's imagery as a defender and guide past the natural presence.

3. The Bird of prey: Image of Sun based Power and Help from above:
3.1. Old Egypt: Horus and the Bird of prey:
In antiquated Egyptian folklore, the bird of prey, especially the Peregrine Hawk, is related with Horus, the divine force of the sky and majesty. Horus is frequently portrayed with the top of a hawk, stressing the bird's association with sun based power and help from above. The bird of prey's sharp visual perception and quick flight are representative of Horus' watchfulness and capacity to answer difficulties quickly.

3.2. The Ashanti: The Sankofa Bird and Immortality:
Among the Ashanti nation of West Africa, the Sankofa bird, frequently portrayed as a hawk, represents the significance of gaining from the past. The bird is depicted with its head turned in reverse while conveying an egg on its back, implying recovering significant information from history. The Sankofa bird of prey fills in as an aide, empowering people to draw shrewdness from their underlying foundations and history.

3.3. The Hawk in Berber Custom: Sunlight based Imagery:
In Berber folklore, the hawk is related with sunlight based imagery. The bird is viewed as a portrayal of the sun's groundbreaking power, underlining the recurrent idea of life and the sun's part in supporting the earth. The hawk's trip across the sky is an image of the sun's excursion, conveying with it topics of reestablishment, warmth, and imperativeness.

4. The Vulture: Purifier and Image of Recovery:
4.1. Old Egypt: Nekhbet and the Vulture:
In old Egyptian folklore, the vulture is related with Nekhbet, a defensive divinity frequently portrayed as a vulture. Nekhbet is viewed as a gatekeeper of Upper Egypt and an image of maternal insurance. The vulture's job in the folklore of antiquated Egypt features its relationship with purging, assurance, and the regenerative patterns of life.

4.2. The Vulture in Shona Folklore: Otherworldly Purging:
Among the Shona nation of Southern Africa, the vulture is viewed as a hallowed bird with critical otherworldly ramifications. The bird is related with otherworldly purging and is accepted to have the capacity to filter and safeguard against negative powers. The vulture's presence is viewed as an image of recharging and the expulsion of profound pollutants.

4.3. Vulture in Yoruba Custom: Change and Astuteness:
In Yoruba folklore, the vulture is connected to change and astuteness. The bird is related with the Orisha Ogun, a god related with iron, war, and change. The vulture's rummaging nature is viewed as a representation for the extraordinary interaction, transforming passing and rot into new life. The vulture exemplifies the pattern of life and passing and the insight acquired through these cycles.

5. The Owl: Gatekeeper of Mysteries and Progress:
5.1. Ashanti Custom: The Owl and Anansi the Insect:
In Ashanti legends, the owl is firmly connected with Anansi, the joke artist bug. The owl fills in as a watchman of Anansi's privileged insights, representing the bird's job in keeping stowed away information and secrets. The owl's nighttime nature adjusts it to the inconspicuous domains and the progress among constantly, life and passing.

5.2. The Owl in Zulu Folklore: An Aide in The great beyond:
Among the Zulu public, the owl is accepted to direct spirits to the great beyond. The bird's hooting is viewed as a sign of the spirit's protected entry to the profound domain. The owl's job as an aide in life following death highlights its association with the concealed and its importance in working with changes between various conditions.

5.3. The Owl in Swahili Folklore: Image of Shrewdness and Assurance:
In Swahili folklore, the owl is related with shrewdness and security. The bird is accepted to have information on both the noticeable and undetectable universes, making it an insightful and watchful watchman. The owl's presence is viewed as a defensive power, averting vindictive spirits and directing people through the intricacies of life.

6. Bird Divination: Looking for Direction from the Avian Domain:
6.1. Divination Practices: Prognostication and Bird Signs:
Divination is a typical practice in numerous African societies, and birds frequently assume a focal part in these customs. Divination, the act of deciphering the way of behaving of birds, is used to acquire experiences into the future, get direction, or pursue significant choices. Explicit bird ways of behaving, like the bearing of flight or the kinds of calls, are accepted to pass on messages from the profound domain.

6.2. The Holy Ibis in Divination: Antiquated Egyptian Practices:
In old Egypt, the Hallowed Ibis was loved for its job in divination. The bird's way of behaving, especially its searching exercises along the Nile Stream, was firmly seen to make expectations about the rural cycle and different parts of life. The Sacrosanct Ibis filled in as a living prophet, giving direction through its regular activities.

6.3. The Job of Owls in Divination Practices: Association with the Soul World:
Owls are much of the time related with divination rehearses across different African societies. The locating or calls of owls are deciphered as messages from the soul world, and seers might utilize such events to offer bits of knowledge into the difficulties or open doors people might experience. The owl's job as a middle person between the seen and concealed makes it a strong image in divinatory customs.

7. Difficulties and Preservation: Adjusting Folklore and Natural Worries:
7.1. Dangers to Sacrosanct Birds: Preservation Difficulties:
Regardless of the social worship for specific birds, many face dangers to their populaces because of territory misfortune, environmental change, and other ecological tensions. The test lies in adjusting the social meaning of these birds with the requirement for preservation measures to safeguard their territories and guarantee their endurance. Cooperative endeavors are vital for address these difficulties while regarding the sacrosanct connections among birds and the networks that hold them dear.

7.2. Protection Drives: Coordinating Native Information:
Endeavors to ration holy birds should coordinate native information and points of view. At times, nearby networks effectively partake in protection drives, attracting on conventional insight to illuminate supportable practices. Cooperative tasks that include both protection specialists and native networks add to a comprehensive methodology that regards social legacy while shielding biodiversity.

4.3   Australian Aboriginal Dreamtime: The Rainbow Serpent and its connection to birds

Australian Native Dreamtime, otherwise called the Dreaming or Jukurrpa, is a hallowed and complex idea that envelops the profound convictions, creation stories, and social legacy of Native Australians. At the core of Dreamtime stories is the Rainbow Snake, a strong and early stage being whose presence pervades the scenes and waters of Australia. This investigation dives into the imagery of the Rainbow Snake and its significant associations with birds inside the rich embroidered artwork of Australian Native Dreamtime.

1. The Dreamtime: Grandiose Creation and Otherworldly Substance
1.1. Figuring out the Dreamtime:

In Australian Native cosmology, the Dreamtime addresses an immortal and otherworldly aspect that coincides with the regular truth of Native people group. It isn't only a previous time however an everlasting domain where familial creatures molded the land, laid out regulations, and made the pith of life. The Dreamtime stories are gone down through oral customs, workmanship, and functions, filling in as a manual for grasping the interconnectedness of every living thing.

1.2. Creation Stories: The Rainbow Snake's Rise:

Key to numerous Dreamtime stories is the Rainbow Snake, an otherworldly and complex being that assumed a urgent part in the production of the world. The Rainbow Snake is related with water, ripeness, and the molding of scenes, making it a crucial power in the Dreaming accounts of different Native gatherings.

2. The Rainbow Snake: Grandiose Watchman and Maker
2.1. Imagery of the Rainbow Snake:

The Rainbow Snake is in many cases portrayed as a titanic and serpentine animal, with a shining, brilliant skin that summons the shades of the rainbow. This imagery reaches out past simple feel; it connotes the snake's association with water, rainbows, and the nurturing powers of the Earth. The Rainbow Snake is both a maker and a destroyer, epitomizing the patterns of life, passing, and recovery.

2.2. Water and Ripeness: The Snake's Basic Power:

Water is a vital component in the imagery of the Rainbow Snake. Its developments across the land, framing streams, waterholes, and lakes, are accepted to be answerable for the production of water sources. Along these lines, the snake's process turns into an imperative power in supporting life, guaranteeing richness in the land and its occupants.

2.3. Shape-moving and Change: The Snake's Ease:

The Rainbow Snake isn't bound to a particular structure. It has the capacity to shape-shift, changing from a serpentine animal into different indications. This ease represents the always changing nature of the Dreamtime and the flexibility expected for endurance in the assorted scenes of Australia.

3. The Rainbow Snake and Avian Associations
3.1. Birds as Couriers and Friends:

Inside the Dreamtime accounts, birds are frequently depicted as couriers, partners, and appearances of the Rainbow Snake's quintessence. These avian associations add profundity to the imagery of the snake, underlining its effect on different parts of the regular world, including the bird species found across Australia.

3.2. The Snake and the Birds of the Sky:

The Rainbow Snake's relationship with birds is complex. In some Dreamtime stories, birds are made by the snake, every species conveying an exceptional importance in the more extensive story. The snake's impact stretches out to the skies, connecting it to the padded occupants that cross the divine domain.

4. Explicit Avian Associations in Dreamtime Stories
4.1. The Crow and the Snake's Melody:

In some Dreamtime stories, the Crow is portrayed as a friend of the Rainbow Snake. The snake is said to have shown the Crow how to sing, and consequently, the Crow went about as a courier for the snake, conveying its melodies and stories to various pieces of the land. This affiliation highlights the snake's job as a bestower of information and the Crow's job as a courier between various Dreamtime domains.

4.2. The Emu and the Snake's Way:

The Emu is one more bird firmly connected to the Rainbow Snake in Dreamtime stories. The winding ways made by the snake's development across the land are said to look like the unmistakable tracks of the Emu. This association isn't just emblematic yet in addition conveys reasonable importance, as Emu tracks are in many cases involved by Native Australians as navigational markers and guides.

4.3. The Jaybird Goose and Water Creation:

In some Dreamtime stories, the Jaybird Goose is related with the making of water sources by the Rainbow Snake. The snake's developments are said to have made the earth break, permitting water to stream and frame waterways and lakes. The Jaybird Goose, in this specific circumstance, turns into an image of the snake's nurturing powers and its effect on the scene.

5. Customs, Craftsmanship, and Emblematic Articulation
5.1. Customs and Functions: Respecting the Snake and Birds:
The Rainbow Snake and its avian associations are respected in different Native
customs and functions. These occasions frequently include melody, dance, and
representative workmanship that portray the snake's excursion and its relationship with
birds. The functions act as a way for networks to interface with the Dreamtime, offer
thanks for the snake's gifts, and guarantee the proceeded with concordance between
the regular and otherworldly universes.

5.2. Imaginative Portrayals: Portraying Dreamtime Associations:
Native Australian workmanship is a strong mode for communicating Dreamtime stories
and the interconnections between the Rainbow Snake and birds. Lively works of art,
rock workmanship, and other visual structures catch the pith of the snake's
developments, its avian associates, and the consecrated scenes formed by its
presence. These creative portrayals act as a scaffold between the profound and the
unmistakable, permitting the narratives to persevere through visual articulation.

6. The Snake's Job in Social Practices
6.1. Preservation and Land Stewardship: The Snake's Inheritance:
The otherworldly meaning of the Rainbow Snake stretches out to contemporary Native
land the executives rehearses. Numerous Native people group view themselves as
overseers of the land, answerable for saving the normal equilibrium molded by the
Dreamtime. The Rainbow Snake's inheritance motivates an all encompassing way to
deal with preservation, where the prosperity of the land is unpredictably attached to
social personality and profound convictions.

6.2. Natural Stewardship: Gaining from the Snake:
The Dreamtime stories highlighting the Rainbow Snake and its avian associations
bestow illustrations of ecological stewardship. The snake's job in molding scenes and
supporting life highlights the significance of protecting biological systems and keeping
an agreeable relationship with the regular world. Native people group attract on these
lessons to advocate for reasonable practices and biological equilibrium.

7. Difficulties and Versatility: Protecting Dreamtime Associations
7.1. Disturbances to Customary Practices:
Colonization and the following interruptions to Native lifestyles have presented
difficulties to the protection of Dreamtime customs. The burden of outer frameworks,
social assignment, and natural changes have undermined the coherence of Native
profound practices. Notwithstanding these difficulties, numerous networks stay versatile,
effectively attempting to recover and rejuvenate their social legacy.

7.2. Cooperative Methodologies: Adjusting Preservation and Culture:

Endeavors to safeguard Dreamtime associations, incorporating those with the Rainbow Snake and birds, frequently include cooperative methodologies. Native drove protection drives, social renewal projects, and associations with non-Native substances expect to adjust the safeguarding of social legacy with more extensive preservation objectives. These drives perceive the interconnectedness of social practices, otherworldly convictions, and natural stewardship.

Chapter 5
Birds in Religious Texts

Birds have caught the human creative mind for centuries, rousing wonder, veneration, and a feeling of the heavenly. Across different strict practices, birds are woven into the texture of hallowed texts, fantasies, and otherworldly lessons. This investigation digs into the rich embroidery of avian imagery and importance in strict messages from assorted societies and beliefs, disentangling the examples, allegories, and heavenly messages conveyed by these winged creatures.

1. Presentation: The Pervasiveness of Birds in Strict Symbolism
1.1. Birds as Images of Greatness:
The pervasiveness of birds in strict texts rises above social and geological limits. Representing opportunity, greatness, and profound association, birds frequently act as couriers between the natural and the heavenly. Their flight, melodies, and ways of behaving are pervaded with significant implications that reverberation across the hallowed sacred texts of the world.

1.2. Representations of Flight and Taking off: Profound Rising:
The demonstration of flight, with its height over the earthbound domain, is a strong illustration for profound rising in numerous strict customs. Birds, as experts of the sky, epitomize the spirit's excursion towards higher insights, illumination, and fellowship with the consecrated. This subject of rising is repetitive in strict stories, delineating the human journey for an association with the heavenly.

2. Birds in Christianity: Couriers, Images, and Heavenly Appearances
2.1. The Bird: A Widespread Image of Harmony:
In Christian imagery, the pigeon is an omnipresent and strong portrayal of harmony and heavenly presence. The pigeon includes conspicuously in the Holy book, quite in the narrative of Noah's Ark, where a bird conveying a peace offering represents the finish of the flood and God's contract with humankind. The Essence of God is likewise frequently portrayed as a bird, plummeting upon Jesus during his submersion.

2.2. The Falcon: Image of Heavenly Assurance and Recharging:
The bird, with its great flight and sharp vision, is an image of heavenly security and recharging in Christian symbolism. In the Songs, the falcon is compared to God, underlining the defensive and caring nature of the heavenly.

The picture of the bird's restoration through shedding has been deciphered as a representation for profound resurrection.

2.3. The Peacock: Restoration and Everlasting status:
In a few Christian practices, the peacock is related with restoration and eternality. The peacock's capacity to supplant its quills represents the recharging of life, and its lively plumage is viewed as an impression of the greatness of God. The peacock is likewise connected to the idea of everlasting life in Christian iconography.

2.4. Birds in Anecdotes and Lessons: Examples from Nature:
Birds every now and again show up in the stories and lessons of Jesus, offering profound illustrations drawn from nature. The illustration of the mustard seed, for instance, looks at the development of the Realm of God to a little mustard seed that develops into a huge tree where birds track down cover. This illustration underscores the groundbreaking force of confidence and the inclusivity of God's realm.

2.5. The Chicken: Image of Alertness and Restoration:
The chicken holds importance in Christianity, especially regarding the narrative of Peter's refusal of Jesus. The crowing of the chicken fills in as a sign of Peter's pass in confidence yet in addition turns into an image of alertness, contrition, and the chance of profound revival. The chicken's crowing imprints a fresh start and the beginning of otherworldly mindfulness.

3. Birds in Islam: Images of God's Creation and Indications of Direction
3.1. The Hoopoe: A Courier in the Quran:
In Islam, the hoopoe (hudhud in Arabic) is referenced in the Quran as a courier to Solomon, giving insight about the Sovereign of Sheba. The hoopoe's job delineates the interconnectedness of all creation and the acknowledgment of creatures as conveyors of heavenly messages. The Quran stresses the signs in nature as impressions of God's insight and direction.

3.2. The Crane: Image of Appreciation and Watchfulness:
In Islamic custom, the crane is related with appreciation and carefulness. The tale of the hoopoe and the insects in the Quran depicts the crane as one of the birds accumulated by Solomon, stressing the significance of appreciation for God's endowments. The crane's watchfulness likewise represents the requirement for devotees to stay cautious in their confidence.

3.3. The Bird of prey: Image of Quickness and Accuracy:
The bird of prey is referenced in Islamic writing as an image of quickness, accuracy, and the significance of involving one's abilities in the help of God.

The Prophet Muhammad is accounted for to have adulated the hawk for its characteristics, drawing otherworldly illustrations from the bird's qualities. The hawk's spryness turns into an illustration for the devotee's excursion toward honorableness and accommodation to God.

3.4. Birds as Signs and Signs: Perusing the Normal World:
In Islam, noticing birds and other normal peculiarities is energized for the purpose of considering God's creation and looking for indications of heavenly direction. Birds are viewed as signs (ayat) in the normal world, and their way of behaving is now and again deciphered as signs or messages from God. This training lines up with the more extensive Islamic perspective that considers the regular world to be an impression of God's insight and signs.

4. Birds in Hinduism: Divine Vehicles, Couriers, and Images of the Spirit
4.1. Garuda: The Hawk as a Heavenly Vehicle:
In Hinduism, Garuda, a legendary hawk, fills in as the vahana (vehicle) of Master Vishnu. Garuda is an image of force, speed, and heavenly help. The picture of Vishnu riding on Garuda addresses the vast request and the victory of dharma (uprightness). Garuda is additionally venerated for his job in bringing the nectar of everlasting status, the amrita.

4.2. Swan and Brahminy Kite: Imagery of Separation and Separation:
The swan (hamsa) and the Brahminy kite (garud) are images of separation and separation in Hindu way of thinking. The swan is said to can isolate milk from water, representing the acumen expected to recognize the everlasting and the transient. The Brahminy kite, related with Garuda, addresses the separation expected for profound acknowledgment.

4.3. Peacock: Vehicle of Kartikeya and Image of Vanity:
The peacock is related with Kartikeya, the child of Shiva, in Hindu folklore. While the peacock is respected for its excellence and relationship with Kartikeya, its vanity is additionally featured in specific accounts. The shedding of quills and the utilization of noxious substances by the peacock act as allegories for defeating pride and inner self.

4.4. Birds as Couriers and Signs: Experiences from the Normal World:
In Hinduism, birds are at times seen as couriers or signs, giving bits of knowledge into future occasions or offering direction. The presence or conduct of explicit birds might be deciphered as signs from the heavenly or impressions of enormous powers. Noticing birds is viewed as a method for acquiring otherworldly bits of knowledge and lining up with the rhythms of nature.

5. Birds in Buddhism: Imagery of Opportunity, Care, and Change
5.1. The Swan: Image of Immaculateness and Profound Rising:
In Buddhism, the swan is an image of immaculateness and profound rising. The picture of a swan floating across the water without getting wet is utilized figuratively to convey rehearsing care and drawing in with the world without being snared by it. The swan's capacity to take off out of sight addresses the freedom of the spirit.

5.2. The Peacock: Change and Illumination:
In Buddhism, the peacock represents change and the potential for illumination. The lively plumage of the peacock is viewed as a representation for the brilliant characteristics that can arise through profound practice. In a few Buddhist customs, the peacock is related with the bodhisattva Avalokiteshvara, addressing sympathy and the easing of misery.

5.3. The Owl: Image of Astuteness and Wisdom:
The owl is viewed as an image of shrewdness and wisdom in Buddhist lessons. The owl's capacity to see plainly in obscurity is utilized figuratively to feature the significance of developing knowledge and grasping despite life's difficulties. The owl turns into an aide in exploring the intricacies of presence.

5.4. Birds in Jataka Stories: Moral Illustrations from Avian Stories:
Jataka stories, accounts of the Buddha's past lives, frequently include birds as focal characters conveying moral examples. These stories utilize the way of behaving and properties of birds to delineate excellencies like sympathy, liberality, and magnanimity. The narratives act as anecdotes, welcoming reflection on moral direct and the way to illumination.

6. Birds in Sikhism: Images of Commitment, Opportunity, and Heavenly Elegance
6.1. The Bird: Image of Commitment and Agreement:
In Sikhism, the bird is related with lowliness, commitment, and the soul of give up to the heavenly will. The delicate and serene nature of the pigeon lines up with Sikh lessons on modesty and sympathy. Master Nanak, the pioneer behind Sikhism, utilized the representation of the pigeon to convey the characteristics of a genuine fan.

6.2. The Falcon: Image of Opportunity and Heavenly Viewpoint:
The bird is referenced in Sikh sacred text as an image of opportunity and the capacity to transcend common worries. Master Gobind Singh, the 10th Sikh Master, is some of the time portrayed with a hawk, connoting the characteristics of solidarity, fortitude, and a point of view that rises above natural constraints. The hawk's flight turns into a representation for the spirit's excursion toward freedom.

6.3. Birds in Sikh Songs: Representations for Otherworldly States:

Sikh songs, known as Gurbani, frequently use bird analogies to convey otherworldly states and yearnings. Birds like the falcon, parrot, and mynah are utilized to outline characteristics like centered fixation, upbeat articulation of commitment, and care. These representations improve the lovely and scrutinizing parts of Sikh sacred text.

7. Birds in Native and Society Religions: Familial Spirits and Natural Couriers
7.1. Local American Practices: The Hawk and Otherworldly Vision:

In numerous Local American practices, the hawk is a hallowed and respected image. The bird is related with profound vision, direction, and an association with the heavenly. Bird feathers are much of the time utilized in functions and customs, representing the presence of genealogical spirits and the transmission of endowments.

7.2. African Folklore: Birds as Couriers and Defenders:

In different African legends, birds assume assorted parts as couriers, defenders, and images of otherworldly understanding. The Southern Ground Hornbill is respected in certain societies as a courier of the predecessors, while the vulture is related with cleansing and recovery. The profound meaning of birds is woven into the texture of day to day existence and ceremonial practices.

7.3. Birds in Shinto: Couriers of Kami and Holy Images:

In Shinto, the conventional religion of Japan, birds are viewed as couriers of kami, the heavenly spirits. The Yatagarasu, a three-legged crow, is a legendary bird in Shinto imagery, addressing direction and help from above. Birds are likewise highlighted in Shinto workmanship and ceremonies, representing the holy association between the natural and the heavenly.

5.1   Biblical references to birds: The dove and the raven in the story of Noah's Ark

The tale of Noah's Ark, tracked down in the Book of Beginning inside the Book of scriptures, is perhaps of the most famous story in Western strict customs. At its center, the story is one of heavenly judgment, human submission, and the commitment of restoration. Key to the story are the birds — explicitly, the pigeon and the raven — that assume essential parts in passing on messages and representing trust, direction, and the unfurling of God's arrangement. This investigation dives into the scriptural references to these birds, disentangling the layers of significance inside the setting of Noah's Ark.

1. The Setting of Noah's Ark: Divine Judgment and Restoration
1.1. The Devilishness of Mankind:

The narrative of Noah's Ark is arranged in a setting of far reaching debasement and mischievousness among humankind. As per Beginning 6:5-8, God notices the degeneration of human profound quality and makes plans to carry a flood to scrub the earth. In the midst of this background, Noah, an honorable man, tracks down favor according to God, and it is to Noah that the heavenly arrangement for salvation is uncovered.

1.2. God's Contract with Noah:

In Beginning 6:9-22, God educates Noah to assemble an ark to save himself, his family, and delegates of every sort of living animal from the approaching flood. This ark turns into a vessel of salvation, and the contract God lays out with Noah represents both heavenly judgment and the commitment of recharging — a pledge fixed with the indication of the rainbow.

2. The Ark and the Birds: Couriers of Trust and Direction
2.1. The Job of Birds in the Ark:

As Noah and his family, alongside sets of creatures, enter the ark, the presence of birds becomes indispensable to the unfurling story. Birds are picked not just for their portrayal of different types of life yet additionally as couriers that will assume urgent parts in deciding the state of the earth after the floodwaters subside.

2.2. The Bird and the Raven: Differentiating Images:

Two explicit birds, the pigeon and the raven, become the dominant focal point in the scriptural record. These birds, however particular in their attributes, act as images with differentiating implications, mirroring the intricacies of heavenly correspondence, human compliance, and the unfurling of God's arrangement.

3. The Raven: A Sign of the Unexplored world
3.1. The Sending of the Raven: Beginning 8:6-7:

In Beginning 8:6-7, as the floodwaters retreat, Noah sets a raven free from the ark to investigate the circumstances outside. The raven, known for its searching nature and capacity to flourish in different conditions, turns into a messenger into the unexplored world. Its trip over the waters and its inability to return promptly make a demeanor of vulnerability.

3.2. The Raven's Absence of Direction:

Not at all like the bird, which turns into an image of trust and direction, the raven doesn't get back to Noah.

Its takeoff and nonappearance from the account leave Noah and his family without clear data about the condition of the earth. The raven, in this unique situation, addresses the cryptic and flighty parts of the regular world, stressing the restrictions of specific types of heavenly correspondence.

4. The Pigeon: Image of Trust and Heavenly Direction
4.1. The Main Sending of the Pigeon: Beginning 8:8-9:
Following the takeoff of the raven, Noah conveys a pigeon to investigate the circumstances outside the ark. The pigeon, known for its tenderness and relationship with virtue, turns into an image of trust and heavenly direction. In Beginning 8:8-9, the bird gets back to the ark, unfit to track down a spot to rest its feet — a sign that the earth is as yet covered by water.

4.2. The Second Sending of the Bird: Beginning 8:10-11:
After seven days, Noah conveys the bird once more, and this time it gets back with an olive leaf in its mouth. This is a crucial second in the story, as the olive leaf flags the subsiding of the floodwaters and the development of dry land. The bird's fruitful return turns into an image of trust, recharging, and the satisfaction of God's commitment.

4.3. The Third Sending of the Bird: Beginning 8:12:
After an additional seven days, Noah conveys the bird again, and this time, the pigeon doesn't return. Its nonappearance means the status of the earth for residence and imprints a defining moment in the story. The pigeon, playing had a focal impact in passing on data about the evolving conditions, turns into an image of heavenly direction and the satisfaction of God's arrangement.

5. Imagery and Philosophical Translations
5.1. Conventional Christian Translations:
In Christian philosophy, the narrative of Noah's Ark is frequently deciphered symbolically. The actual ark is viewed as an image of salvation, and the birds — especially the pigeon and the raven — take on emblematic importance. The raven, with its takeoff and absence of return, might be viewed as a portrayal of the vulnerability and inadequacy of common information. Conversely, the pigeon, with its fruitful returns and the conveying of the olive leaf, represents divine direction, trust, and the satisfaction of God's commitments.

5.2. Religious Subjects: Compliance, Persistence, and Restoration:
The tale of the pigeon and the raven inside the bigger story of Noah's Ark includes different philosophical subjects.

Noah's dutifulness to God's directions, the persistence showed in the sit tight for the subsiding of the floodwaters, and a definitive recharging of the earth all add to the more extensive philosophical message of heavenly provision, pledge, and the chance of reclamation after a time of preliminary.

6. Examples and Applications

6.1. Divine Direction and Persistence:

The story of the pigeon and the raven confers illustrations about divine direction and the significance of tolerance in sitting tight for God's timing. The pigeon, addressing trust and heavenly confirmation, instructs that even in testing conditions, there is a commitment of recharging and satisfaction. Persistence, exhibited by Noah's pausing and the successive sendings of the birds, turns into an excellence integral to the unfurling of God's arrangement.

6.2. The Intricacy of Heavenly Correspondence:

The differentiating encounters of the pigeon and the raven additionally feature the intricacy of heavenly correspondence. While the pigeon's profits give clear messages of trust and evolving conditions, the raven's flight leaves Noah and his family in a condition of vulnerability. This intricacy welcomes reflection on the secrets of heavenly direction and the acknowledgment that a few parts of God's arrangement may not be quickly clear or fathomable.

7. Social and Abstract Impacts

7.1. Social Effect and Emblematic Portrayal:

Past its strict importance, the narrative of Noah's Ark and the birds significantly affects social and creative articulations. The bird, specifically, has turned into an all inclusive image of harmony and trust, rising above strict limits. The account has propelled innumerable masterpieces, writing, and music, with the birds filling in as powerful images that resound with subjects of endurance, restoration, and the persevering through human soul.

7.2. Scholarly and Imaginative Works: Motivations from Noah's Ark:

Abstract works, like sonnets, books, and youngsters' accounts, frequently draw motivation from the narrative of Noah's Ark and the birds. Specialists since the beginning of time have portrayed the location of the pigeon getting back with the olive leaf, catching the profound and representative profundity of the scriptural story. The getting through reverberation of this story in the social and imaginative circles verifies its ageless subjects and widespread allure.

5.2   Quranic symbolism: The hoopoe bird in Surah Al-Naml

Surah Al-Naml, otherwise called "The Insects," is the 27th section of the Quran, and it holds an unmistakable spot in Islamic sacred writing because of its rich story content and significant imagery. Among the captivating components inside Surah Al-Naml is the notice of the hoopoe bird (hudhud in Arabic), an animal presented with remarkable characteristics and importance with regards to divine correspondence. This investigation digs into the Quranic imagery of the hoopoe bird, disentangling its part in Surah Al-Naml and the examples it gives.

1. Setting of Surah Al-Naml: A Story of Solomon's Realm
1.1. Outline of Surah Al-Naml:

Surah Al-Naml is a part that winds around together different stories, and one of its focal subjects rotates around the realm of Prophet Solomon (Sulaiman in Arabic). The surah examines Solomon's insight, his collaborations with various animals, and the acknowledgment of heavenly signs in the regular world. Inside this more extensive setting, the hoopoe bird arises as a huge player in the unfurling story.

1.2. Solomon's Correspondence with Creatures: An Exceptional Gift:

As per Islamic practice, Solomon had the capacity to speak with creatures and grasp their dialects. This special gift was an indication of the heavenly blessings conceded to him. The Quranic account depicts Solomon as an equitable and insightful ruler whose domain reached out over people, jinn, and the set of all animals.

2. The Hoopoe's Excursion: Looking for Data
2.1. Quranic Section: Surah Al-Naml (27:20-28):

The Quranic section in regards to the hoopoe is found in Surah Al-Naml, explicitly in refrains 27:20-28. In these sections, the hoopoe sets out on an excursion to carry data to Solomon about a far off land controlled by the Sovereign of Sheba (Bilqis in Arabic). The hoopoe's process turns into a crucial component in the surah, starting a succession of occasions that disentangle the insight of Solomon and the accommodation of different animals to God's arrangement.

2.2. Hoopoe's Perceptions: Perceiving the Sovereign's Realm:

The hoopoe, flying over the land, notices the Sovereign of Sheba's prosperous realm. It takes note of the lavishness of her royal residence, her strong lofty position, and the faithfulness of her kin to the sun, which was a typical worshipful practice around then. The hoopoe's sharp perceptions structure the reason for its report to Solomon, filling in as a channel for correspondence between the creature world and the human prophet.

3. Imagery of the Hoopoe in Surah Al-Naml
3.1. Intelligence and Correspondence:
The hoopoe in Surah Al-Naml fills in as an image of shrewdness and compelling correspondence. By embraced the excursion to assemble data and passing it on to Solomon, the hoopoe exhibits a comprehension and mindfulness that rises above its instinctual conduct. This imagery supports the more extensive subject of heavenly insight penetrating the regular world and the interconnectedness of all animals in the heavenly arrangement.

3.2. Accommodation to God's Orders:
The hoopoe's dutifulness to Solomon's order to convey a message to the Sovereign of Sheba highlights the subject of accommodation to God's orders. In Islamic philosophy, creation, including creatures, is all viewed as intrinsically in a condition of accommodation (Islam in Arabic) to God's will. The hoopoe, through its activities, embodies this condition of accommodation, recognizing Solomon as a prophet and courier of God.

3.3. Acknowledgment of Heavenly Signs:
The hoopoe's sharp perceptions of the Sovereign of Sheba's realm and individuals' worshipful practices feature its capacity to perceive and demonstrate the veracity of heavenly signs in the regular world. In Islam, the idea of Ayat (signs) is focal, accentuating the presence of God's signs in creation for the people who reflect and contemplate. The hoopoe turns into an observer to the indications of God's creation and a member in passing these signs on to Solomon.

3.4. Modesty and Administration:
The hoopoe's part in Surah Al-Naml is additionally emblematic of modesty and administration. Notwithstanding its little size and apparently unimportant status contrasted with the greatness of Solomon's realm, the hoopoe assumes a critical part in the unfurling story. This imagery highlights the Quranic subject that importance lies not in superficial presentations but rather in the genuineness of one's activities and accommodation to God's will.

4. Illustrations and Reflections
4.1. The Meaning of Perception:
The hoopoe's perceptions of the Sovereign of Sheba's realm accentuate the significance of sharp perception in grasping our general surroundings. In Islam, reflection (tafakkur) is exceptionally supported, and the regular world is viewed as a book of heavenly signs. The hoopoe, as an onlooker, turns into a member in uncovering the indications of God's creation.

4.2. The Job of Creatures in God's Arrangement:
The Quranic depiction of Solomon's capacity to speak with creatures challenges human-driven points of view and accentuates the basic job of creatures in God's arrangement. The hoopoe, alongside different animals, turns into a channel for divine correspondence, exhibiting the interconnectedness of all living creatures in their accommodation to God.

4.3. Shrewdness in Humble Structures:
The decision of the hoopoe, a little and genuine bird, as the courier in this story highlights the Quranic topic that shrewdness can appear in humble and apparently common structures. It challenges assumptions about the wellsprings of astuteness and reminds adherents to be available to getting direction from unforeseen quarters.

5. Social and Imaginative Portrayals
5.1. Impact on Islamic Workmanship and Writing:
The account of the hoopoe in Surah Al-Naml has affected Islamic workmanship and writing from the beginning of time. The bird is in many cases portrayed in Islamic small scale compositions and enlightened original copies, representing astuteness, correspondence, and accommodation to heavenly will. The account has additionally roused writers and narrators, who draw upon the imagery of the hoopoe in conveying moral and profound illustrations.

5.2. Contemporary Understandings:
In the contemporary setting, researchers, journalists, and specialists keep on investigating the imagery of the hoopoe in Surah Al-Naml. Contemporary translations might draw associations between the hoopoe's excursion and the difficulties of looking for information and shrewdness in the advanced world. The bird's job might be viewed as a similitude for the significance of correspondence and figuring out across different societies and social orders.

5.3 Buddhist and Jain traditions: The mythical Garuda and its role in religious texts

The legendary Garuda, an unbelievable animal in Hindu, Buddhist, and Jain customs, fills in as an image of solidarity, opportunity, and greatness. While frequently connected with Hindu folklore, the Garuda's importance stretches out past Hinduism into the domains of Buddhism and Jainism, every custom mixing its own interesting translations into the story. This investigation dives into the legendary Garuda and its multi-layered job in strict texts, especially inside the settings of Buddhist and Jain practices.

1. Garuda in Hindu Folklore: An Outline
1.1. Iconography and Properties:
In Hindu folklore, the Garuda is an unbelievable bird-like animal and the mount (vahana) of Ruler Vishnu, one of the primary divinities in the Hindu pantheon. Garuda is normally portrayed as a sublime bird or hawk with a brilliant body, huge wings, and a snout and claws sufficiently strong to convey the heaviness of the god. The Garuda is many times depicted fighting against snakes, representing the victory of heavenly powers over bedlam.

1.2. Imagery in Hinduism:
The Garuda holds profound imagery in Hinduism, addressing a few ethics, including strength, dedication, and the ability to conquer impediments. As Ruler Vishnu's mount, Garuda implies the heavenly power that conveys the god on his vast excursions, stressing the reliance and amicable connection among divine beings and their creature sidekicks.

2. Garuda in Buddhist Practice: Imagery and Change
2.1. Mix into Buddhist Cosmology:
In Buddhist customs, the Garuda takes on remarkable aspects, frequently coordinated into the cosmological and legendary system. The Mahayana Buddhist custom, specifically, consolidates components from pre-Buddhist and non-Buddhist social settings, adjusting them to convey Buddhist lessons.

2.2. The Garuda in Jataka Stories:
Jataka stories, stories relating the past existences of the Buddha, highlight the Garuda as a person in different structures. These stories utilize the Garuda's credits to convey moral examples and Buddhist ethics. The Garuda's connections with different creatures, like nagas (snakes), give figurative accounts that investigate subjects of empathy, altruism, and the extraordinary force of Buddhist practice.

2.3. Garuda in Mahayana Sutras:
Certain Mahayana sutras, hallowed texts in Mahayana Buddhism, likewise consolidate the Garuda as a representative figure. In these messages, the Garuda might address the extraordinary force of edification or the capacity to rise above the limits of common presence. The bird's capacity to take off uninhibitedly through the sky turns into a representation for the freed mind that rises above the patterns of misery and resurrection.
2.4. Garuda in Tibetan Buddhism: Defensive Imagery:
In Tibetan Buddhism, the Garuda is frequently connected with security and is portrayed as a gatekeeper figure.

Garuda's pictures might embellish strict relics, sanctuaries, and ceremonial carries out, representing a defensive power against adverse impacts and snags on the profound way. In this unique situation, the Garuda turns into a wild and watchful gatekeeper of the Dharma.

3. Garuda in Jain Custom: A Symbol of Peacefulness
3.1. Exceptional Translation in Jainism:
In Jainism, an old Indian strict custom stressing peacefulness (ahimsa) and otherworldly parsimony, the Garuda takes on an unmistakable job. While Jainism doesn't consolidate divinities similarly as Hinduism, it coordinates fanciful figures, including the Garuda, into its stories with remarkable understandings lined up with Jain standards.

3.2. Peacefulness and Conjunction:
In Jain cosmology, the Garuda is viewed as a generous figure, typifying the standards of peacefulness and concurrence. Not at all like the Garuda in Hindu folklore, which is much of the time depicted in struggle with snakes, the Jain Garuda is agreeable and non-forceful. This understanding lines up with Jain lessons that underscore empathy for every living being, advancing a dream of conjunction as opposed to a showdown.

3.3. Garuda in Jain Craftsmanship and Imagery:
Jain craftsmanship frequently portrays the Garuda in a peaceful and quiet way, mirroring the Jain obligation to ahimsa. The bird might be highlighted in models and creative portrayals inside Jain sanctuaries, filling in as a sign of the significance of sympathy and the evasion of damage to any living being.

4. Garuda's All inclusive Imagery: Subjects Across Customs
4.1. Opportunity and Greatness:
Across Hindu, Buddhist, and Jain customs, the Garuda reliably represents opportunity and greatness. Whether as the mount of Master Vishnu, a person in Buddhist stories, or an image of peacefulness in Jainism, the Garuda's capacity to take off above natural imperatives addresses the desire for otherworldly freedom and greatness past the patterns of birth and passing.

4.2. Change and Illumination:
In Mahayana Buddhism, the Garuda fills in as an image of change and illumination. Its consideration in different sutras and Jataka stories highlights its relationship with the extraordinary force of Buddhist practice. The Garuda's job in these stories turns into a similitude for the potential for significant inward change and profound arousing.

4.3. Defensive Energy:

In both Hindu and Tibetan Buddhist customs, the Garuda encapsulates defensive energy. Whether monitoring Ruler Vishnu or filling in as a defensive figure in Tibetan Buddhism, the Garuda is worshipped for its capacity to avert negative powers and snags. This defensive imagery supports its job as a watchman and partner on the profound excursion.

5. Examples and Reflections

5.1. Peacefulness and Conjunction:

In the Jain translation, the Garuda's portrayal as a figure of peacefulness and conjunction offers a significant example. It highlights the Jain obligation to ahimsa and fills in as a sign of the significance of agreeable living with all creatures. The Garuda turns into an image of empathy and regard for life in its different structures.

5.2. Interconnectedness of Customs:

The Garuda's presence in Hindu, Buddhist, and Jain practices mirrors the interconnectedness of strict and social stories in the Indian subcontinent. The flexibility of the Garuda's imagery across these customs features the common social legacy and the smoothness with which legendary figures can rise above unambiguous strict limits.

5.3. Goals for Freedom:

The general imagery of the Garuda reverberates with the common human yearning for freedom and profound greatness. Whether with regards to Hindu dedication, Buddhist illumination, or Jain peacefulness, the Garuda turns into an image that rises above partisan contrasts, exemplifying the immortal human mission for independence from misery and the limits of everyday presence.

6. Social Articulations and Imaginative Portrayals

6.1. Imaginative Portrayals:

Imaginative portrayals of the Garuda have large amounts of the social articulations of Hindu, Buddhist, and Jain customs. Sanctuaries, figures, works of art, and compositions frequently include the famous picture of the Garuda. The imaginative renderings catch the bird's great structure and convey the emblematic lavishness related with its job in strict stories.

6.2. Custom and Reflection Practices:

In Hinduism, the Garuda is adored in different customs and celebrations. Lovers might offer supplications and perform services devoted to Garuda, looking for the bird's favors for insurance and otherworldly prosperity.

Likewise, in Tibetan Buddhism, the Garuda's defensive imagery is woven into customs and services, upgrading the profound feeling of sanctuaries and religious communities.

Chapter 6
Birds of War and Wisdom

Birds, with their smooth flight and mysterious presence, have long caught the human creative mind. Across societies and developments, birds have been invested with representative importance, addressing a bunch of subjects going from war and struggle to intelligence and greatness. This investigation digs into the rich embroidered artwork of social accounts, folklores, and strict practices that component birds as strong images of both warlike ability and significant insight.

1. Presentation: Plumes on the War zone and in the Corridors of Astuteness
1.1. The Double Idea of Birds:
Birds, with their capacity to navigate the skies and occupy both natural and heavenly domains, exemplify a duality that reverberates with different human encounters. This investigation centers around two significant parts of avian imagery — the portrayal of birds as images of war, struggle, and power, and their job as transporters of intelligence, illumination, and greatness.

1.2. Widespread Allure:
The imagery of birds isn't bound to a solitary culture or strict practice; rather, it traverses the globe, reflecting shared human encounters, goals, and fears. From the falcons of antiquated Rome to the vultures of Hindu folklore, and from the ravens of Norse legends to the cranes of East Asian customs, birds act as adaptable images that rise above social limits.

2. Birds of War: Plumes on the Combat zone
2.1. The Hawk: Image of Majestic Power and War

2.1.1. Roman Hawk:
In old Rome, the hawk was an image of majestic power and military may. The Roman armies conveyed the aquila, a bronze hawk standard, into fight, connoting the power of the Roman state. The deficiency of the aquila was a grave disrespect, and its recuperation involved most extreme significance, mirroring the cozy association between the hawk and the military personality of Rome.

2.1.2. Bald Eagle: American Imagery:
Additionally, the bald eagle has turned into a persevering through image of the US, addressing opportunity and strength.

The hawk is noticeably highlighted in American iconography, including the Incomparable Mark of the US, where it grasps bolts and a peace offering, connoting the country's availability for war and its craving for harmony.

2.2. The Vulture: Image of Death and Reestablishment
2.2.1. Hindu Folklore: The Garuda and the Nagas:

In Hindu folklore, the Garuda, an unbelievable bird, is frequently connected with war and struggle. As the mount of Master Vishnu, Garuda takes part in fights against snakes, representing the grandiose battle among request and turmoil. The vulture, a bird frequently connected with death, turns into a strong image of recharging and grandiose equilibrium.

2.2.2. Egyptian Vulture: Scrounger on the War zone:

The Egyptian vulture, known for its searching propensities, was available on antiquated combat zones, benefiting from the remaining parts of fallen fighters. This relationship with death and rot prompted the vulture being connected to war and its outcome in different societies.

2.3. The Raven: Sign of War and Destiny
2.3.1. Norse Folklore: Odin's Ravens:

In Norse folklore, the raven holds an unmistakable spot as a harbinger of war and an image of Odin, the lord of war and shrewdness. Odin's two ravens, Huginn (thought) and Muninn (memory), fly across the world to accumulate data and carry fresh insight about the combat zone to the god. The raven's presence is viewed as a sign of approaching clash and the certainty of destiny.

2.3.2. Celtic Culture: Fight Goddess and Ravens:

In Celtic culture, ravens were related with the fight goddess Morrigan. These birds were accepted to be couriers of war and passing, their presence on the combat zone connoting the goddess' contribution in the issues of humans.

3. Birds of Shrewdness: Plumage of the Astute
3.1. The Owl: Image of Intelligence and the Mysterious

3.1.1. Greek Folklore: Athena's Owl:

In Greek folklore, the owl is related with Athena, the goddess of shrewdness. The owl turned into an image of intelligence and information, and its presence was accepted to be an indication of Athena's direction. The bird's nighttime nature and its capacity to find in obscurity added to its relationship with the mysterious and secret information.

3.1.2. Local American Societies: Owl as an Aide:

Different Local American societies likewise view the owl as an image of intelligence. In certain customs, the owl is viewed as an aide that assists people with exploring the profound domains. Its sharp insight and quiet flight make it an image of instinct and inward sight.

3.2. The Crane: Image of Life span and Edification

3.2.1. East Asian Customs: Cranes in Chinese and Japanese Craftsmanship:

In Chinese and Japanese craftsmanship and folklore, the crane is venerated for its class and life span. The Red-delegated Crane, specifically, is an image of favorable luck and illumination. In East Asian customs, collapsing 1,000 paper cranes is accepted to bring best of luck and satisfaction of wishes.

3.2.2. Hinduism: Saraswati's Peacock:

In Hinduism, the peacock is related with Saraswati, the goddess of information and shrewdness. The peacock's superb plumage represents the dynamic and bright parts of learning, craftsmanship, and writing.

3.3. The Swan: Image of Immaculateness and Profound Rising

3.3.1. Hinduism: Saraswati's Swan:

In Hinduism, the swan is related with Saraswati also. The swan is accepted to can isolate milk from water, representing acumen and the quest for genuine information. The bird's white plumage addresses virtue and profound climb.

3.3.2. Celtic Folklore: Swans in Irish Fables:

In Celtic folklore, swans are frequently connected with change and excellence. The Offspring of Lir, an impactful Irish fantasy, recounts the tale of four kin transformed into swans because of a revile. Their swan structure turns into an image of perseverance, excellence, and the repetitive idea of presence.

4. Birds as Middle people: Couriers Between Universes

4.1. Ravens and Crows: Transports of Heavenly Messages

4.1.1. Norse Folklore: Odin's Couriers:

In Norse folklore, Odin's ravens, Huginn and Muninn, act as couriers between the god and the human domain. Their trips across the world represent the progression of data and heavenly knowledge. The ravens are loved as consecrated mediators, overcoming any issues between the sky and the natural space.

4.1.2. Local American Customs: Crow as a Courier:

In different Local American customs, the crow is viewed as a courier between the physical and profound domains. Its cawing is accepted to pass on messages from the soul world, filling in as an aide for those sensitive to its representative language.

4.2. The Gooney bird: Image of Heavenly Revenge and Reclamation
4.2.1. Scholarly Imagery: Coleridge's "The Rime of the Old Sailor":

In writing, the gooney bird is an image of both heavenly revenge and reclamation. Samuel Taylor Coleridge's sonnet "The Rime of the Old Sailor" investigates the results of killing a gooney bird, depicting the bird as a harbinger of both destruction and inevitable salvation.

4.2.2. Sea Legend: Strange notions about Gooney bird:

Sailors generally saw the gooney bird with a blend of wonderment and fear. Killing a gooney bird was viewed as misfortune, and the bird's presence was accepted to safeguard mariners on their excursions across the immense and unusual oceans.

5. Social Effect and Creative Articulations
5.1. Workmanship and Writing: Portrayals of Birds in Human Creative mind

5.1.1. Visual Expressions: Portrayals of Birds in Canvases and Figures:

Specialists since forever ago have been dazzled by the imagery of birds, integrating them into artistic creations, models, and different types of visual articulation. The superb bird, savvy owl, and rich swan have become persevering through themes, conveying a scope of implications and feelings.

5.1.2. Abstract Works: Birds as Images in Verse and Composition:

Scholars and artists have woven avian imagery into the texture of their abstract works. From Shakespeare's utilization of the crow in "Macbeth" to Tennyson's lovely investigation of the gooney bird in "The Antiquated Sailor," birds act as strong images that bring out both instinctive and magical reactions.

5.2. Strict Practices: Ceremonies and Emblematic Importance
5.2.1. Customs: Bird Imagery in Strict Functions:

In different strict customs, birds assume a part in customs and services. Whether delivered during functions or emblematically addressed in strict craftsmanship, birds become courses for profound importance and supernatural desires.

5.2.2. Representative Importance: Special raised area Pieces and Strict Symbols:
Birds frequently find a spot in strict iconography and raised area pieces. From the
superb falcon representing heavenly capacity to the tranquil swan addressing
otherworldly climb, these emblematic portrayals improve the visual and profound
elements of strict practices.

6. End: Wings of Representative Flight
6.1. The Multi-layered Nature of Bird Imagery:
Bird imagery, with its double nature enveloping both warlike ability and significant
insight, reflects the intricacy of the human experience. From the war zone to the lobbies
of shrewdness, birds have made a permanent imprint on the shared perspective of
assorted societies.

6.2. General Strings and Social Specificities:
While general subjects of opportunity, greatness, and intelligence are woven into avian
imagery, social specificities shape the subtleties of these images. The falcon, respected
in Roman and American societies, takes on various implications in Local American
practices. Essentially, the owl, an image of shrewdness in Greece, conveys
unmistakable implications in Local American legends.

6.3. Progressing Veneration and Variations:
The adoration for birds as images keeps on advancing. In contemporary settings, birds
are adjusted and reconsidered to mirror the changing elements of human idea and
cultural qualities. From ecological protection endeavors motivated by the crane to
contemporary writing investigating the emblematic meaning of birds, these animals
proceed to rouse and direct mankind.

7. Last Contemplations: The Persevering through Trip of Emblematic Birds
In the tremendous and various embroidery of human imagery, birds take off as strong
couriers, encapsulating the range of human encounters. Whether rising above the war
zone as images of warlike may or roosted in the domain of shrewdness and amazing
quality, birds rise above the restrictions of their actual presence to become images that
resound across societies, religions, and ages. In the wings of these representative
birds, mankind finds a common language that addresses the desires, fears, and
immortal desires of the human soul.

6.1   Roman mythology: The owl as a symbol of wisdom

In the rich embroidery of Roman folklore, the owl arises as a strong image of shrewdness, premonition, and secret. Related with the goddess Minerva, the Roman partner of the Greek goddess Athena, the owl rises above its nighttime nature to turn into a worshipped and mysterious figure in the pantheon of Roman divinities. This investigation digs into the multi-layered job of the owl in Roman folklore, unwinding its emblematic importance, social reverberation, and getting through presence as a padded prophet of shrewdness.

1. Presentation: Minerva and the Confounding Owl
1.1. Minerva: Roman Goddess of Intelligence:

Minerva, the Roman goddess of shrewdness, war, and human expression, possesses a conspicuous spot in Roman folklore. As the partner of the Greek goddess Athena, Minerva exemplifies acumen, vital ability, and imaginative articulation. The owl, as Minerva's holy buddy, turns into a meaningful image that rises above the nighttime domain to epitomize the goddess' relationship with insight.

1.2. Social Reverberation of the Owl:

The owl's relationship with insight isn't bound to folklore alone; it saturates Roman culture, impacting craftsmanship, writing, and cultural discernments. The owl's baffling look and nighttime exercises add to its persona, making it a strong image that reverberates past the bounds of strict stories.

2. Minerva and the Owl: A Fanciful Organization
2.1. Starting points of Minerva: The Goddess' Introduction to the world:

Minerva's starting points in Roman folklore are entwined with a phenomenal birth. As indicated by the fantasy, she sprang completely developed and protected from the head of Jupiter, the lord of the divine beings. This interesting birth featured her heavenly parentage and set up for her job as a goddess of outstanding insight and keenness.

2.2. Minerva and the Challenge with Neptune:

A critical episode in Minerva's legendary story includes a challenge among her and Neptune, the lord of the ocean, for the support of the city of Athens. The divine beings were entrusted with introducing a gift to the residents, and Minerva, with her insight, offered the olive tree. Neptune, conversely, hit the ground with his harpoon, delivering a saltwater spring. The residents picked Minerva's gift, stressing the worth of insight and quiet pursuits over the tumult related with the ocean.

2.3. The Owl as Minerva's Friend: Shrewdness in Plumes:

Vital to Minerva's iconography is the owl, which fills in as her dependable friend. The owl's presence highlights the goddess' relationship with intelligence, as owls have for quite some time been images of prescience and sharp discernment. The decision of the owl as Minerva's sidekick lines up with the Roman appreciation for the bird's baffling and nighttime characteristics.

3. Imagery of the Owl: Shrewdness Past the Evening
3.1. Nighttime Shrewdness: The Owl's Variations:

The owl's nighttime propensities, sharp vision, and capacity to explore in murkiness add to its emblematic relationship with astuteness. In Roman folklore, the owl's ability to see what others can't turns into a representation for Minerva's scholarly understanding and the quest for information that rises above the limits of the noticeable.

3.2. The Owl as a Manual for the Hidden world:

Notwithstanding its relationship with astuteness, the owl is in some cases connected to the domain of the dead and the hidden world. This association adds a layer of secret to the bird's imagery, proposing its job as an aide between the universe of the living and life following death. The owl's puzzling nature lines up with the secrets and secret information related with the domain of the dead.

3.3. Owls in Roman Craftsmanship and Engineering: Portrayals of Shrewdness:

In Roman craftsmanship and engineering, portrayals of Minerva frequently incorporate the owl, stressing the goddess' association with astuteness. The owl's presence in models, reliefs, and coins fills in as a visual sign of Minerva's scholarly ability and the social worth put on shrewdness in Roman culture.

4. Social Respect and Convictions
4.1. Owl Signs and Prognostications: Divination through Quills:

The Romans, in the same way as other old societies, rehearsed divination, looking for direction from the regular world to decipher signs and signs. Owls, with their nighttime presence and secretive disposition, were in many cases considered signs related with shrewdness and prescience. The perception of owl conduct, flight examples, and vocalizations turned into a method for deciphering the heavenly will.

4.2. Owls in Roman Writing: Representative Accounts:

Roman writing, including verse and philosophical works, consolidates the imagery of the owl to convey more profound implications. Artists and rationalists draw upon the owl's nighttime nature and Minerva's relationship with intelligence to investigate subjects of information, knowledge, and the quest for scholarly edification.

5. Owl Cliques and Sanctuaries: Commitment to Minerva
5.1. Cliques and Celebrations: Regarding Minerva and the Owl:
Minerva had devoted religions and celebrations all through the Roman Realm, where
admirers gave recognition to the goddess of shrewdness. The owl, as Minerva's
sacrosanct sidekick, probable assumed an emblematic part in these strict observances,
further hardening the bird's relationship with the goddess and the excellencies she
encapsulated.

5.2. Sanctuaries and Safe-havens: Engineering Articulations of Shrewdness:
Sanctuaries committed to Minerva frequently highlighted owl symbolism in engineering
components, building up the association between the goddess and the representative
owl. These safe-havens became actual exemplifications of the social love for
astuteness and scholarly pursuits, welcoming admirers to look for Minerva's direction in
their academic undertakings.

6. Tradition of the Owl in Roman Culture
6.1. Phonetic Heritage: Astuteness in Words:
The owl's imagery reaches out into the semantic domain, impacting the Latin language
and its demeanors. Expressions, for example, "be careful the owl around evening time"
became phrases forewarning against misleading and secret risks, mirroring the owl's
double nature as an image of intelligence and expected premonition.

6.2. Owl Themes in Roman Ancient rarities: Regular Insight:
Past sanctuaries and landmarks, owl themes tracked down their direction into regular
Roman life. From coins to family things, the owl's presence in ancient rarities addresses
its getting through imagery and the joining of Minerva's insight into the texture of Roman
culture.

7. The Persevering through Presence of the Owl: A Representative Continuum
7.1. Progress to Christianity: Variations and Changes:
As Christianity step by step displaced customary Roman convictions, the imagery of the
owl endured, though with changes. In Christian workmanship, owls held their
relationship with shrewdness however took on extra layers of importance, in some
cases addressing cautiousness and watchfulness.

7.2. Middle age and Renaissance Recoveries: Resurgence of Imagery:
During the middle age and Renaissance periods, old style imagery encountered a
recovery. The owl, with its connections to antiquated astuteness, reemerged in
craftsmanship, writing, and heraldry. Craftsmen and researchers drew motivation from
old style themes, adding to the owl's proceeded with presence in social articulations.

6.2   Celtic mythology: The role of crows and ravens in battle

In the rich embroidery of Celtic folklore, the presence of crows and ravens is profoundly entwined with topics of fight, prediction, and astuteness. These strange and shrewd birds, frequently portrayed as couriers of the divine beings, hold an unmistakable spot in Celtic old stories, filling in as signs, guides, and images of both the disorder of war and the insight of the Otherworld. This investigation dives into the multi-layered job of crows and ravens in Celtic folklore, disentangling their representative importance, legendary accounts, and persevering through impact on Celtic social convictions.

1. Presentation: The Mysterious Corvids in Celtic Legend
1.1. The Celtic Perspective: Association with Nature and the Otherworld:
Celtic folklore is well established in the regular world, and creatures, especially birds, are frequently permeated with emblematic importance. Among these animals, crows and ravens stand apart as confounding creatures, crossing over the unremarkable and the supernatural in the Celtic creative mind.

1.2. The Double Idea of Corvids: War and Intelligence:
Crows and ravens, by and large alluded to as corvids, exemplify a double nature in Celtic folklore. On one hand, they are related with the mayhem of fight, searching on the outcome of war. Then again, these birds are connected to insight, prescience, and their puzzling association with the Otherworld — a domain past the customary human experience.

2. The Morrigan: Goddess of War and Destiny
2.1. The Morrigan's Presence: Shape-Moving Goddess:
Fundamental to the relationship of crows and ravens with fight in Celtic folklore is the figure of the Morrigan. The Morrigan is a mind boggling and diverse goddess, frequently portrayed as a shape-shifter who can change into different structures, including that of a crow or raven. She is a watchman of power, a harbinger of war, and a weaver of destiny.

2.2. Fight Goddess: Effect on Fighting:
The Morrigan's presence is especially felt on the war zone, where she is known to shape the result of struggles. As a conflict goddess, she imparts dread in her foes and rouses champions, uplifting the power of fight. The picture of crows and ravens hovering above turns into a sign of looming struggle, with the Morrigan directing the course of war.

2.3. Nurturer of Legends and the Killed: Familial Associations:
In her job as a nurturer, the Morrigan is likewise connected with the brave dead. Crows and ravens, as her representative couriers, are accepted to accompany the spirits of fallen champions to the Otherworld. This double part of the Morrigan as both a power of obliteration in fight and a manual for the great beyond delineates the intricacy of Celtic convictions encompassing fighting and the pattern of life and demise.

3. Cu Chulainn and the Crows: A Hero's Sign
3.1. Cu Chulainn: Chivalrous Figure of Irish Folklore:
In the Ulster Pattern of Irish folklore, the unbelievable legend Cu Chulainn experiences the impact of crows in an essential snapshot of his life. Cu Chulainn is an imposing champion known for his ability in fight, and his predetermination is entwined with the otherworldly powers that oversee the destiny of legends.

3.2. The Sign of the Crows: Demise Approaches:
In the story of "The Demise of Cu Chulainn," a gathering of crows plummets upon the legend as he participates in battle. The crows' presence is deciphered as a sign flagging Cu Chulainn's looming death. This association between the corvids and the legend's destiny builds up the confidence in the private connection between fight, passing, and the secretive powers that administer predetermination.

4. Intelligence and Prescience: Wheat the Favored
4.1. Wheat the Favored: Raven-related Legend:
In Welsh folklore, the figure of Grain the Favored is firmly connected with ravens. Wheat, a monster and courageous lord, is known for his insight and association with the Otherworld. His name, "Wheat," really signifies "raven" in Welsh, accentuating the emblematic job of these birds in his account.

4.2. Grain's Excursion to the Otherworld: Shrewdness and Penance:
In the story "Branwen, Girl of Llyr," Grain leaves on an excursion to the Otherworld. During his time in the Otherworld, he experiences significant insight and finds out about his own destiny. Grain's relationship with ravens is featured when, upon his demise, his head is cut off and turns into a prophet, talking expressions of prescience. The ravens assume a crucial part in this enchanted association, connecting the legend's insight to the ethereal domain.

5. The Cailleach and Her Corvid Mates
5.1. The Cailleach: Old Witch and Winter Goddess:
In Scottish and Irish fables, the Cailleach is an old and strong figure related with winter, power, and change.

While not unequivocally a conflict goddess, the Cailleach's association with the corvids adds a layer of secret and imagery to her personality.

5.2. The Corvids as Couriers: Transports of Insight:
In certain stories, the Cailleach is joined by crows and ravens, filling in as couriers between the commonplace world and the Otherworld. The corvids' part in conveying messages and working with correspondence highlights their association with the concealed domains and the insight of the Cailleach.

6. Social Adoration and Representative Practices
6.1. Divination and Sign Perusing: Corvids as Guides:
In Celtic societies, the perception of corvid conduct was in many cases deciphered as a type of divination. The flight examples, calls, and ways of behaving of crows and ravens were accepted to pass on messages from the Otherworld and deal bits of knowledge into what's in store. Druids, the profound heads of antiquated Celtic social orders, were especially sensitive to these signs.

6.2. Imagery in Workmanship and Writing: Portrayals of Corvids:
Celtic workmanship and writing frequently highlight portrayals of crows and ravens, underscoring their emblematic significance. Whether woven into embroideries, cut into stone, or portrayed in enlightened compositions, the corvids' presence fills in as a visual indication of their legendary importance and social reverberation.

7. Heritage and Present day Translations
7.1. Present day Old stories and Social Congruity:
The imagery of crows and ravens in Celtic folklore keeps on resounding in present day legends and social articulations. The puzzling and clever nature of these birds continues in contemporary stories, adding to their getting through appeal as images of both conflict and shrewdness.

7.2. Protection and Natural Mindfulness: Saving the Holy Birds:
In a few present day translations, endeavors are made to associate the veneration for corvids in Celtic folklore with natural preservation. The consciousness of the significance of these birds in environments and their representative importance in Celtic societies adds to drives pointed toward saving their living spaces and guaranteeing their proceeded with presence in the normal world.

6.3   East Asian martial arts: Crane and hawk symbolism in warrior culture

East Asian hand to hand fighting, well established in a rich social and philosophical legacy, frequently draw motivation from the normal world.

Among the heap images implanted in combative techniques customs, the crane and bird of prey arise as strong and worshipped representations. These birds, with their unmistakable qualities, epitomize a double embodiment that mirrors the agreeable mix of shrewdness, elegance, and fierceness — a combination that resounds in the way of thinking, methods, and social articulations of East Asian hand to hand fighting. This investigation digs into the imagery of the crane and falcon in East Asian combative techniques, unwinding their importance, fanciful roots, and getting through impact on champion culture.

1. Presentation: Nature as a Wellspring of Motivation
1.1. The Crossing point of Combative techniques and Nature: Concordance and Equilibrium:

Key to East Asian combative techniques reasoning is the idea of congruity and equilibrium, and nature fills in as a significant wellspring of motivation. The effortless and strong developments of creatures, particularly birds, are frequently incorporated into hand to hand fighting procedures, mirroring a profound appreciation for the normal world and its standards.

1.2. Imagery in Hand to hand fighting: Past Actual Procedures:

Hand to hand fighting in East Asia reach out past actual battle; they envelop a comprehensive way to deal with self-awareness, underlining mental discipline, moral qualities, and profound development. The imagery of creatures, for example, the crane and bird of prey, adds layers of significance to these military customs, offering specialists a structure for grasping their specialty and its more extensive ramifications.

2. The Crane in East Asian Hand to hand fighting: Elegance and Astuteness
2.1. Legendary Roots: Crane as an Image of Everlasting status:

The crane, loved for its style and life span, holds a critical spot in East Asian folklore. In Chinese old stories, the crane is related with everlasting status and heavenly creatures. The legendary Xian, or Daoist immortals, are much of the time portrayed riding on cranes, accentuating the bird's association with the otherworldly domain.

2.2. Crane Style Kung Fu: Copying Elegance and Accuracy:

In hand to hand fighting, especially in styles like White Crane Kung Fu (Bai He Quan), the developments of the crane are copied to develop beauty, equilibrium, and accuracy.

Specialists of Crane Style Kung Fu look to reflect the smoothness and balance of the crane, coordinating these characteristics into their strategies. The crane's wings, mouth, and claws move a different scope of strikes, blocks, and equivocal moves.

2.3. Wing Chun: The Agile Specialty of the Crane:
Wing Chun, a famous Chinese military craftsmanship, is said to integrate components of the crane's developments. The accentuation on responsiveness, concurrent assault and safeguard, and the idea of diversion in Wing Chun line up with the qualities credited to the crane. This combination of the crane's quintessence upgrades the workmanship's adequacy and stylish allure.

2.4. Japanese Combative techniques: The Crane in Aikido:
In Japanese combative techniques, Aikido, a discipline zeroed in on diverting a rival's power, draws motivation from the developments of the crane. The accentuation on roundabout movements, mixing with a rival's energy, and keeping a quiet community line up with the characteristics related with the crane. Aikido experts try to encapsulate the crane's insight and versatility.

3. The Falcon in East Asian Hand to hand fighting: Speed and Fierceness
3.1. Sell Imagery: Speed, Concentration, and Accuracy:
While the crane typifies beauty and intelligence, the bird of prey addresses speed, concentration, and savagery. In East Asian societies, the falcon's savage nature and sharp vision make it an image of accuracy and quick activity. The falcon's capacity to lock onto its prey with immovable center turns into a similitude for the champion's focus and conclusiveness.

3.2. Korean Combative techniques: The Bird of prey in Hwa Rang Do:
Hwa Rang Do, a Korean military workmanship with profound verifiable roots, consolidates the bird of prey as an image of speed and accuracy. The military craftsmanship's methods, techniques, and ways of thinking draw motivation from the falcon's hunting ability. Experts of Hwa Rang Truly do plan to develop the bird of prey's characteristics, mixing them with mental mettle and moral standards.

3.3. Japanese Hand to hand fighting: Falcon propelled Methods in Karate:
In Japanese hand to hand fighting, especially in disciplines like Karate, the falcon's qualities track down articulation in different methods. The attention on dangerous speed, direct strikes, and exact developments mirrors the impact of the bird of prey's savage nature. The falcon turns into an emblematic aide for professionals trying to upgrade their military ability.

4. Hand to hand fighting Way of thinking: Mixing Crane's Insight and Bird of prey's Accuracy

4.1. Yin and Yang: Adjusting Contradicting Powers:

The imagery of the crane and bird of prey is much of the time figured out from the perspective of Yin and Yang, the philosophical idea of adjusting restricting powers. The crane, addressing Yin, epitomizes characteristics of receptivity, shrewdness, and ease. Interestingly, the falcon, addressing Yang, represents decisiveness, speed, and accuracy. Military specialists endeavor to incorporate these apparently restricting characteristics, looking for an agreeable equilibrium that improves their viability on both physical and otherworldly levels.

4.2. Flexibility and Adaptability: Crane-Bird of prey Combination:

Professionals of East Asian hand to hand fighting perceive the significance of flexibility and adaptability. By epitomizing the characteristics of both the crane and the falcon, military specialists expect to explore various circumstances with astuteness, elegance, speed, and accuracy. This union takes into consideration a dynamic and liquid way to deal with battle, mirroring the consistently changing nature of military experiences.

5. Social and Philosophical Effect

5.1. Harmony Buddhism: Care and Presence:

The imagery of the crane and bird of prey is profoundly interwoven with Harmony Buddhism, which has affected East Asian combative techniques. Harmony lessons stress care, presence, and the coordination of physical and mental viewpoints. The effortless, reflective developments motivated by the crane and the engaged, definitive activities propelled by the bird of prey line up with Harmony standards, encouraging a comprehensive way to deal with military practice.

5.2. Bushido: The Method of the Champion:

In Japan, the Samurai embraced Bushido, the "Method of the Champion," as a set of principles that stretched out past military procedures. The standards of Bushido, including integrity, fortitude, consideration, regard, genuineness, honor, and dedication, track down reverberation in the imagery of the crane and bird of prey. The insight of the crane and the accuracy of the bird of prey are incorporated into the moral structure that administers the Samurai's lifestyle.

6. Imagery in Hand to hand fighting Symbolism and Relics

6.1. Images and Badge: Crane and Bird of prey Themes:

In hand to hand fighting, images, emblem, and school logos frequently consolidate crane and falcon themes. These images act as visual portrayals of the qualities and characteristics that professionals try to typify.

The rich outline of a crane or the wild look of a falcon turns into a powerful sign of the more profound implications implanted in combative techniques practice.

6.2. Weapons and Structures: Crane and Bird of prey Procedures:
Hand to hand fighting structures, or individualized structure, oftentimes integrate methods enlivened by the crane and bird of prey. Weapon structures, specifically, feature the liquid and exact developments related with the crane, as well as the quick and centered strikes motivated by the falcon. Weapons like the staff, mirroring the crane's lengthened neck, and the katana, exemplifying the bird of prey's accuracy, become expansions of the military craftsman's appearance.

7. Present day Understandings and Worldwide Impact
7.1. Globalization of Combative techniques: Crane and Bird of prey Around the world:
As East Asian combative techniques have spread worldwide, the imagery of the crane and falcon has risen above social limits. Specialists from assorted foundations embrace these images, finding general reverberation in the standards they address. The crane's insight and the falcon's accuracy have become getting through guides for military specialists around the world, molding the ways of thinking and procedures of different disciplines.

7.2. Mainstream society: Crane and Falcon Prime examples:
The imagery of the crane and falcon saturates mainstream society, from combative techniques movies to writing and visual expressions. These original birds frequently show up as themes in accounts of bravery, discipline, and self-revelation. Characters typifying the beauty of the crane or the savagery of the bird of prey resound with crowds, adding to the persevering through charm of these images.

Chapter 7
Modern Interpretations and Adaptations

In the unique scene of the advanced world, the practices and images of the past go through consistent reevaluation and variation. This liquid interaction is obvious across assorted spaces, from workmanship and writing to innovation and theory. In this investigation, we dive into the complex domain of present day understandings and variations, analyzing how social, creative, and mechanical articulations go through change while exploring the strain among custom and advancement.

1. Presentation: Custom in Motion
1.1. The Consistently evolving Embroidery:
As social orders advance, so do the accounts, images, and practices that characterize their social personality. Present day translations and transformations act as a scaffold between the rich embroidery of custom and the steadily changing elements of contemporary life. This mind boggling dance between the past and the current shapes the social awareness, affecting how we see, draw in with, and rehash our common legacy.

1.2. The Double Idea of Variation: Conservation and Change:
Variation is a nuanced interaction that includes both protection and change. It requires a comprehension of the center components that characterize a custom while considering development and reevaluation. Whether in the domains of craftsmanship, writing, innovation, or social practices, the harmony between protecting the embodiment of custom and embracing change is a fragile dance that mirrors the intricacies of our interconnected world.

2. Current Understandings in Workmanship and Writing
2.1. Rethinking Exemplary Works: Abstract Transformations:
Writing, an immortal storehouse of human articulation, much of the time goes through reevaluation and transformation. Exemplary works are rethought through various social focal points, giving new viewpoints on recognizable stories. For instance, William Shakespeare's plays find new life in variations like "West Side Story," translating the immortal subjects of affection and struggle to a cutting edge setting.

2.2. Visual Expressions: Remixing Custom in Contemporary Workmanship:
Contemporary specialists frequently draw motivation from conventional structures, reshaping them to reflect present day sensibilities. This pattern is apparent in crafted by specialists who mix conventional artistic creation procedures with computerized media or integrate social images into provocative establishments. By remixing custom, craftsmen add to a discourse between the past and the present, cultivating a unique trade of thoughts.

2.3. Film and TV: Adjusting Stories for a Worldwide Crowd:
Film and TV transformations assume an essential part in acquainting conventional stories with a worldwide crowd. Whether it's a reevaluation of an exemplary novel or a cutting edge take on a social legend, visual narrating has the ability to rise above borders. For example, the Indian awe-inspiring "Mahabharata" has been adjusted into different realistic structures, reverberating with crowds around the world.

3. Social Works on: Protecting Legacy in a Contemporary Setting
3.1. Customary Expressions and Specialties: Reviving Legacy:
Customary expressions and specialties, frequently imperiled by the tensions of modernization, experience a recovery through imaginative transformations. Craftsmans might inject conventional stoneware with contemporary plans, protecting the craftsmanship while speaking to current preferences. This convergence of custom and advancement revives social practices that could somehow blur into indefinite quality.

3.2. Celebrations and Ceremonies: Contemporary Articulations of Custom:
Celebrations and ceremonies, necessary to social character, go through shifts because of changing cultural standards. Present day understandings of customary services might integrate new components, making them more comprehensive or applicable to contemporary worries. Adjusting customs guarantees their coherence while permitting networks to develop with the times.

3.3. Language and Vernacular: Exploring Phonetic Variation:
Language, a transporter of social legacy, faces the test of adjusting to the requests of the cutting edge world. Vernacular dialects might develop to integrate new jargon connected with innovation, globalization, and changing social designs. Adjusting semantic variation jelly social extravagance while working with correspondence in a quickly changing etymological scene.

4. Innovation and Advancement: Adjusting to the Computerized Age
4.1. Advanced Restorations: Virtual Exhibition halls and Files:
In the advanced age, social curios are not bound to actual spaces. Historical centers
and files tackle innovation to make virtual displays, permitting individuals overall to
remotely investigate social legacy. This transformation democratizes admittance to
social fortunes and guarantees their protection despite actual disintegration.

4.2. Gamification of Custom: Protecting Legacy Through Play:
Computer games give a novel stage to adjusting customary stories and legends. Game
engineers integrate social components into intuitive stories, offering players a vivid
encounter that cultivates an appreciation for assorted customs. This gamification of
custom scaffolds generational holes, making legacy seriously captivating and available.

4.3. Online Entertainment and Social Articulation: A Worldwide Stage:
Online entertainment stages act as unique spaces for the transformation and scattering
of social articulations. Customary artistic expressions, music, and ceremonies track
down new crowds through advanced sharing. Hashtags, challenges, and online
networks become vehicles for social trade, permitting people to draw in with and add to
the continuous story of their legacy.

5. Difficulties and Debates in Current Variation
5.1. Allocation versus Appreciation: Exploring Awarenesses:
The line between social appreciation and allocation is many times obscured in current
transformations. While culturally diverse trade can cultivate understanding, it is
fundamental to explore expected awarenesses and stay away from the commodification
of consecrated customs. Finding some kind of harmony requires a nuanced
comprehension of the social settings included.

5.2. Protection from Change: Adjusting Conservation and Development:
Conservatives might oppose specific transformations, seeing them as a danger to the
validness of their legacy. Adjusting the protection of guiding principle with the
requirement for development represents a test. Discourse and joint effort between
conventional professionals and trend-setters are pivotal to exploring this strain.

6. Globalization and Social Combination: A Blade that cuts both ways
6.1. Social Homogenization: The Disintegration of Variety:
As societies meet on a worldwide scale, there is a gamble of social homogenization,
where unmistakable practices lose their uniqueness notwithstanding predominant
worldwide impacts. Current variations should be aware of saving variety and forestalling
the eradication of interesting social characters.

6.2. Culturally diverse Fertilization: Advancing the Worldwide Embroidery:
On the other hand, globalization works with culturally diverse fertilization, cultivating a rich trade of thoughts, feel, and practices. This interconnectedness can prompt a powerful combination of customs, making crossover shapes that resound with different crowds. The test lies in guaranteeing that this combination is described by common regard and correspondence.

7.1 Contemporary art and literature featuring avian deities

In the domain of contemporary workmanship and writing, a captivating resurgence of avian gods has taken off. Drawing motivation from different legends and social customs, craftsmen and scholars weave accounts that investigate the representative lavishness of birds, imbuing their works with layers of implying that rise above reality. This investigation digs into the energetic scene of contemporary inventiveness, where avian gods take off as images of amazing quality, opportunity, and the persevering through association among mankind and the heavenly.

1. Presentation: The Avian Renaissance
1.1. Legendary Birds in Present day Creative mind:
In the contemporary creative and scholarly scene, there has been an outstanding renaissance of interest in avian gods — legendary birds with divine credits. These gods, frequently depicted as lofty and ethereal winged creatures, act as convincing images that resound with topics of otherworldliness, change, and the inborn human yearning for association with the hallowed.

1.2. Culturally diverse Investigation: Past Limits:
Contemporary makers draw from an immense supply of worldwide legends, embracing avian gods from societies as different as Greek, Egyptian, Norse, Hindu, and Local American. This diverse investigation enhances imaginative articulation as well as highlights the comprehensiveness of the emblematic language of birds in human cognizance.

2. Avian Gods in Contemporary Craftsmanship
2.1. Imagery and Representation: Past Tasteful Allure:
Craftsmen in the contemporary circle influence the imagery and allegorical possible implanted in avian divinities to convey complex accounts and summon significant feelings. Past tasteful allure, these imaginative portrayals act as a visual language that imparts topics of otherworldliness, greatness, and the transaction between the natural and the heavenly.

2.2. Oddity and Avian Iconography: Salvador Dalí's Swan:
Surrealist specialists, known for their investigation of the psyche and fantastical symbolism, frequently integrate avian iconography to inspire fanciful states. Salvador Dalí, a noticeable figure in the Surrealist development, painted "Swans Reflecting Elephants," a work that entwines the pictures of swans and elephants in a dreamlike reflecting. The swan, related with excellence and change, turns into a strong image in Dalí's investigation of the strange and puzzling.

2.3. Contemporary Establishments: Winged Creatures in Metropolitan Spaces:
In contemporary establishments, specialists bring avian gods into metropolitan spaces, changing public conditions into domains of otherworldly thought. Enormous scope models of winged figures, suggestive of antiquated bird gods, welcome watchers to draw in with the extraordinary and think about the crossing point between the heavenly and the ordinary.

3. Scholarly Reverberation: Avian Gods in Contemporary Composition
3.1. Reconsidering Legends: Neil Gaiman's American Divine beings:
Contemporary writing frequently reconsiders old legends, reviving prototype figures. Neil Gaiman's "American Divine beings" is a cutting edge exemplary that winds around together legends from different societies, including Norse folklore. In the novel, Odin, the Norse All-Father, is joined by two ravens, Huginn and Muninn, who act as his couriers. Gaiman's investigation of avian gods in a contemporary setting features their getting through pertinence in the human mind.

3.2. Verse and Avian Purposeful anecdotes: Mary Oliver's Wild Geese:
Artists, as well, track down motivation in the imagery of birds, utilizing avian purposeful anecdotes to investigate subjects of opportunity, self-disclosure, and the interconnectedness of every single living being. Mary Oliver's sonnet "Wild Geese" welcomes perusers to ponder the profound examples presented by wild geese in flight. The symbolism of these relocating birds turns into an illustration for the human excursion, encouraging people to embrace their position in the immense and interconnected embroidery of presence.

3.3. Supernatural Authenticity and Avian Accounts: Haruki Murakami's Kafka on the Shore:
In the domain of supernatural authenticity, avian imagery takes on extraordinary aspects. Haruki Murakami's "Kafka on the Shore" includes a person who can speak with felines and encounters a dreamlike experience with a magical, talking crow. The crow turns into an aide and an image of greatness, obscuring the limits between the unremarkable and the mysterious in Murakami's story.

4. Model Importance: The Phoenix in Contemporary Workmanship and Writing

4.1. Phoenix Revived: Reestablishment and Change:

The phoenix, a legendary bird related with resurrection and recharging, holds getting through bid in contemporary workmanship and writing. Craftsmen and essayists frequently summon the phoenix as an image of strength, greatness, and the repetitive idea of life. Its model importance reverberates across societies and keeps on moving imaginative articulations that investigate subjects of change and the victory of the human soul.

4.2. Visual Craftsmanship and the Phoenix: Image of Perseverance:

Contemporary visual craftsmen much of the time portray the phoenix in different mediums, from compositions to advanced craftsmanship. The phoenix's blazing resurrection and brilliant plumage become illustrations for individual and aggregate perseverance even with difficulties. These visual portrayals welcome watchers to consider their own ability for restoration and the repetitive idea of life's excursion.

4.3. Writing and the Phoenix: J.K. Rowling's Fawkes:

In writing, the phoenix arises as a strong image in contemporary works. J.K. Rowling's "Harry Potter" series highlights Fawkes, Dumbledore's phoenix buddy. Fawkes' capacity to recuperate through tears and go through searing resurrection lines up with the conventional phoenix folklore. Rowling instills the phoenix with profundity, involving it as an illustration for unwaveringness, penance, and the getting through force of affection.

5. Contemporary Social Developments: Avian Divinities and Character

5.1. Avian Divinities and Character Legislative issues: Native Points of view:

In contemporary social developments, avian divinities have importance in conversations of character and native points of view. For a few Native societies, birds like the falcon and the owl are holy creatures with profound otherworldly associations. Contemporary craftsmen from these networks utilize avian imagery to attest social personality, challenge generalizations, and recover accounts that middle on the holiness of the normal world.

5.2. LGBTQ+ Portrayal: The Gooney bird in Present day Eccentric Writing:

Avian imagery likewise tracks down reverberation in contemporary LGBTQ+ writing, where the gooney bird, a superb seabird, turns into an image of eccentric character and opportunity. This transformation reconsiders the gooney bird's fanciful relationship with weight and revile, transforming it into a strong image of strength and the quest for one's actual self.

6. Advanced Stages and Computer generated Realities: Avian Divinities in the Digital Domain

6.1. Symbols and Robotic Birds: Past the Actual Domain:

As innovation progresses, avian gods track down another environment in computerized stages and augmented realities. Symbols, frequently addressed as winged creatures, explore the internet, representing the combination of the profound and the mechanical. These computerized signs of avian divinities investigate the developing idea of human association and greatness in the advanced age.

6.2. Computer games and Legendary Birds: Excursion and Investigation:

Computer games, as vivid narrating mediums, integrate avian divinities into virtual universes. Games like "Excursion" include legendary birds as guides, driving players through scenes that summon a feeling of marvel and otherworldly investigation. The intelligent idea of computer games permits players to draw in with avian imagery in manners that go past conventional account structures.

7.2   The role of birds in popular culture and folklore

From old legends to contemporary stories, birds have enamored the human creative mind, taking off through the embroidered artwork of societies around the world. In mainstream society and old stories, these padded creatures represent a heap of ideas, from opportunity and greatness to couriers of the heavenly. This investigation digs into the rich and changed job of birds in forming the stories of mainstream society and legends, exhibiting their getting through importance as images, sidekicks, and analogies.

1. Birds as Images of Opportunity and Greatness

1.1. Hawk: The Image of Opportunity:

The hawk, with its superb wingspan and sharp vision, has for some time been an image of opportunity and power in different societies. In the US, the bald eagle is a notable public image, addressing the country's soul and standards. Its presence on the Incomparable Mark of the US conveys a feeling of freedom, strength, and the quest for a higher vision.

1.2. Gooney bird: A Similitude for Endless Opportunity:

In writing, the gooney bird, known for its huge maritime excursions, turns into an illustration for limitless opportunity. Samuel Taylor Coleridge's sonnet "The Rime of the Old Sailor" includes a gooney bird whose passing brings a revile, featuring the representative weight joined to these superb birds and the outcomes of disturbing the congruity among mankind and the regular world.

1.3. Owl: Shrewdness and Opportunity in Greek Folklore:

In Greek folklore, the owl is related with Athena, the goddess of shrewdness. The owl's capacity to find in obscurity lines up with Athena's trait of foreknowledge. As an image of shrewdness, the owl addresses a type of scholarly opportunity — the capacity to recognize and explore the intricacies of the world.

2. Birds as Couriers and Images of Correspondence
2.1. Transporter Pigeon: Couriers of War and Harmony:

Since forever ago, transporter pigeons play had an imperative influence as couriers, particularly during seasons of war. Their homing impulses and speed made them important for correspondence across significant distances. In mainstream society, the picture of a pigeon conveying a rolled-up message embodies the idea of correspondence defeating hindrances.

2.2. Raven: A Courier in Norse Folklore:

In Norse folklore, ravens are related with Odin, the All-Father. Huginn and Muninn, Odin's ravens, act as couriers, bringing him data from the human domain. The raven's job as a communicator between universes highlights its representative importance as a scaffold between the heavenly and the natural.

2.3. Mockingbird: Image of Mimicry and Correspondence:

In American fables, the mockingbird is praised for its capacity to impersonate the melodies of different birds. This mimicry has prompted the bird turning into an image of correspondence and variation. The book "To Kill a Mockingbird" by Harper Lee utilizes the imagery of the mockingbird to address blamelessness and the significance of understanding and sympathizing with others.

3. Birds as Images of Adoration and Connections
3.1. Lovebirds: Representing Heartfelt Associations:

Lovebirds, little parrots known for areas of strength for framing bonds, have become images of close connections in mainstream society. The picture of two lovebirds settled together addresses getting through affection and friendship. This imagery is in many cases utilized in workmanship, writing, and in any event, wedding topics.

3.2. Swans: Polish and Timeless Love:

Swans are every now and again connected with subjects of affection and style. In various folktales and legends, swans are depicted as images of timeless love and change. Swans framing long lasting pair bonds has saturated social stories, and their smooth presence on waterways inspires a feeling of immortal sentiment.

4. Birds as Signs and Images of Change
4.1. Crow: A Sign in Old stories and Strange notion:
Crows, frequently connected with secret and knowledge, play played parts in fables as signs or couriers from the otherworldly domain. In different societies, the presence of crows is deciphered as an indication of progress, change, or looming occasions. Their dark plumage and rowdy cawing add to the persona encompassing these birds.

4.2. Hummingbird: Image of Strength and Satisfaction:
In Local American old stories, the hummingbird is much of the time seen as an image of euphoria and versatility. Its capacity to float and move quickly between blossoms is related with the quest for joy and the enthusiasm for life's passing minutes. The hummingbird's energetic presence in folklore mirrors its groundbreaking imagery.

4.3. Phoenix: Image of Resurrection and Recharging:
The phoenix, a legendary bird tracked down in different societies, represents resurrection and recharging through its repeating life pattern of death and restoration. In mainstream society, the phoenix is a strong illustration for defeating difficulty and arising more grounded from difficulties. Its blazing resurrection catches the human interest with change and the persevering through trust for recharging.

5. Birds as Social Symbols in Famous Media
5.1. Hedwig in "Harry Potter": Image of Unwaveringness:
In J.K. Rowling's "Harry Potter" series, Hedwig, Harry's pet frigid owl, fills in as both a courier and an image of dependability. Hedwig's demise in the series addresses a deficiency of a sidekick as well as a strong second that highlights the topic of penance and the close to home reverberation that birds can summon in narrating.

5.2. Huge Bird in "Sesame Road": Instructive Buddy:
Huge Bird, the famous person from "Sesame Road," is an enormous, cordial bird that fills in as an instructive ally for youthful watchers. Through its fun loving cooperations and undertakings, Huge Bird epitomizes the positive characteristics related with birds, like interest, fellowship, and a feeling of marvel.

6. Birds in Notions and Social Convictions
6.1. Jaybirds: Old stories and Odd notions:
Jaybirds have a rich presence in old stories and strange notions, particularly in European customs. The rhyme "One for distress, two for delight" mirrors the conviction that the quantity of jaybirds one sees can anticipate future occasions. This notion shows the way that birds, even in their customary experiences, can become woven into the texture of social convictions.

6.2. Strange notions Around Owls: People Convictions and Signs:

Owls, with their nighttime propensities and unmistakable appearances, have been related with odd notions in different societies. In certain customs, owls are viewed as images of shrewdness, while in others, they are viewed as harbingers of destruction. These convictions feature the assorted and now and again disconnected manners by which birds are woven into social stories.

7.3 Environmental and conservation perspectives on birds in mythology

Birds, with their ethereal flights and various species, have involved an unmistakable spot in folklore across societies. Past their representative importance, the accounts and convictions encompassing birds offer significant experiences into mankind's relationship with the normal world. In this investigation, we dive into the ecological and preservation viewpoints implanted in bird folklore, unwinding the insight these antiquated accounts hold for contemporary endeavors to save and safeguard avian life.

1. The Sacrosanct Watchmen of Nature
1.1. Falcon: An Image of Ecological Stewardship:

In different folklores, the falcon frequently holds the job of a gatekeeper soul or god related with the climate. For Local American societies, the hawk is a hallowed bird representing strength, vision, and a profound association with the land. The idea of hawks as defenders highlights the significance of ecological stewardship, passing on a message of veneration for the normal world.

1.2. Garuda in Hindu Folklore: Defender of the Universe:

In Hindu folklore, Garuda, a glorious half-man, half-falcon animal, is worshipped as the mount of Master Vishnu. Garuda's job as a defender reaches out past heavenly domains; he is likewise viewed as a gatekeeper of the climate. This imagery accentuates the interconnectedness of every living being and the obligation people hold as stewards of the Earth.

2. Birds as Harbingers of Natural Changes
2.1. Raven in Local American Legend: Courier of Change:

For Local American societies, the raven is a diverse image related with change and change. Ravens, through their ways of behaving and calls, are accepted to pass on messages about ecological movements. The acknowledgment of birds as harbingers of natural changes highlights the close connection among people and the climate in native viewpoints.

2.2. Gooney bird in Sea Old stories: Signs of Route:
Sea old stories frequently includes birds like the gooney bird as signs of climate and route. Mariners generally accepted that the presence or conduct of specific birds could anticipate storms or demonstrate the closeness of land. These legendary affiliations exhibit an old comprehension of birds as marks of natural circumstances.

3. Birds as Images of Regular Equilibrium
3.1. Owl in Greek Folklore: Attendant of Environmental Congruity:
In Greek folklore, the owl is related with Athena, the goddess of shrewdness. The owl's nighttime propensities and sharp faculties represent carefulness and understanding, characteristics fundamental for keeping up with environmental equilibrium. The love for owls in folklore highlights that the safeguarding of normal concordance requires thinking and a profound comprehension of the climate.

3.2. Crow and Equilibrium in Asian Folklore:
In different Asian legends, crows are frequently connected with the adjusting of vast powers. For instance, in Japanese fables, the Yatagarasu, a three-legged crow, directs the legendary figure Jimmu, the primary sovereign of Japan. The crow's job as an aide and balancer of enormous energies proposes an old affirmation of the fragile harmony in the normal world.

4. Birds as Specialists of Ecological Examples
4.1. Icarus and Natural Pride: A Useful example:
The Greek legend of Icarus, who flew excessively near the sun with wings made of plumes and wax, fills in as a wake up call about ecological pride. Icarus' dismissal for the limits of nature prompts his ruin. This fantasy exemplifies that humankind should perceive and regard the limits set by the normal world to keep away from devastating outcomes.

4.2. The Goose that Laid the Brilliant Eggs: A Story of Ravenousness and Natural Outcomes:
The tale of the goose that laid the brilliant eggs, tracked down in different societies, cautions against uncontrolled avarice and the outcomes of taking advantage of normal assets. The story underlines the significance of reasonable practices and living as one with the climate to guarantee long haul thriving.

5. Preservation and the Imagery of Jeopardized Birds
5.1. The Legendary Phoenix and Preservation Purposeful anecdote:
The phoenix, a legendary bird related with resurrection and restoration, can be seen as a moral story for protection endeavors.

As jeopardized species face the danger of eradication, the idea of 'coming to life through preservation rehearses turns into a strong theme. The phoenix fantasy moves a feeling of trust and versatility even with ecological difficulties.

5.2. Condor in South American Legends: Protection and Social Importance:
In South American legends, the condor holds social importance and is in many cases seen as an image of force and shrewdness. As condor populaces face danger, endeavors to monitor these glorious birds become interwoven with the conservation of social legacy. Preservation drives for imperiled birds take on added importance when the species holds social and fanciful significance.

6. Birds as Inspirations for Biodiversity Preservation
6.1. The Variety of Avian Species: An Impression of Nature's Extravagance:
Folklores frequently include a different exhibit of bird species, mirroring the wealth of the normal world. Perceiving the variety of avian life in fantasies can act as an inspiration for biodiversity protection. Every species, with its novel credits and jobs, adds to the natural equilibrium, underscoring the significance of saving this variety.

6.2. Hummingbirds and Environment Wellbeing: A Preservation Illustration:
In a few native societies, the hummingbird represents flexibility and versatility. Moderates draw motivation from the hummingbird as a representation for tending to ecological difficulties. The bird's capacity to drift and concentrate nectar from various blossoms highlights the significance of flexibility despite evolving biological systems.

7. Current Folklores: Birds in Contemporary Preservation Accounts
7.1. Narrating for Preservation: Penguins in "Spring of the Penguins":
In current narrating, narratives like "Walk of the Penguins" feature the difficulties looked by penguins as they continued looking for endurance. These accounts act as integral assets for preservation, bringing issues to light about the effects of environmental change and human exercises on weak bird species.

7.2. Big names and Protection Missions: The Gooney bird and Plastic Contamination:
Famous people and forces to be reckoned with frequently take part in protection missions to resolve ecological issues. The gooney bird, known for its vulnerability to plastic contamination, turns into an image in these missions, underscoring the requirement for dependable garbage removal and preservation rehearses.

Chapter 8
Conclusion

In the extensive excursion through the domains of folklore, social imagery, and ecological viewpoints, a rich embroidery of subjects has unfurled, uncovering the perplexing associations between human cognizance, narrating, and the regular world. From the dazzling stories of divine beings and legends to the significant imagery of creatures and components, the investigation has traversed different societies, ages, and trains. As we explore the coming full circle parts of this investigation, we end up remaining at the convergence of custom and development, folklore and protection, fashioning a way ahead into the steadily advancing scene of human comprehension.

1. Strings of Shared characteristic Across Societies
1.1. Widespread Originals: Associating Across Existence
One of the striking disclosures in this investigation is the presence of widespread originals that rise above social limits. Whether looking at the legend's excursion, the imagery of birds, or the themes of creation and obliteration, consistent ideas arise, winding around a story that resounds across existence. These originals address a common human encounter, underlining the force of narrating as a binding together power.

1.2. Social Variety: Commending the Embroidery of Humankind
At the same time, the investigation has highlighted the lavishness of social variety. Each fanciful practice, from Greek and Norse to Hindu and Native, delivers one of a kind points of view on the human condition, the universe, and the heavenly. The variety in legends fills in as a demonstration of the versatility of narrating, forming itself as per the social settings and shared mindset of various social orders.

2. Folklore as a Reflection of Human Experience
2.1. Impressions of Mankind: Divine beings and Humans
Folklore, at its center, mirrors the multi-layered nature of the human experience. Through the stories of divine beings and humans, legends and antiheroes, yearnings and hardships, folklore fills in as a mirror that catches the pith of being human. The divine beings exemplify the temperances and indecencies that reverberation in the hearts of humans, filling in as metaphorical aides exploring the intricacies of presence.

2.2. Moral Examples and Moral Predicaments

Inserted inside legends are moral examples and moral situations that rise above their social starting points. The battles of characters like Prometheus, who opposes the divine beings to improve mankind, or Arjuna, defying the moral difficulties of war, welcome thoughtfulness and examination. These stories propel us to wrestle with ageless inquiries of ethical quality, equity, and the results of our decisions.

3. The Representative Language of Folklore
3.1. Imagery as an Informative Medium

Folklore imparts through an emblematic language that rises above the restrictions of exacting understanding. Whether it's the snake in Eden, the lotus in Hindu cosmology, or the phoenix in resurrection accounts, images convey layers of implying that reverberate on close to home, mental, and profound levels. The investigation has unwound the unpredictable semiotics of these images, stressing their ability to convey significant bits of insight past the bounds of regular language.

3.2. Original Images: Scaffolds Between Universes

Prototype images, for example, the excursion of the legend or the inestimable tree, go about as extensions between the commonplace and the extraordinary. These images interface people across societies and ages, framing a common dictionary that addresses the aggregate oblivious. The investigation has enlightened the persevering through meaning of original images, stressing their job as vessels for general insights.

4. The Crossing point of Folklore and Natural Viewpoints
4.1. Birds as Couriers and Natural Markers

The assessment of birds in folklore has given a one of a kind focal point through which to investigate natural and preservation viewpoints. Birds, as couriers and images, convey environmental stories inside legendary customs. From the gooney bird as a sign of route to the falcon as a gatekeeper soul, these legends perceive birds as harbingers of natural changes and transports of biological insight.

4.2. Preservation Moral stories: The Phoenix and Imperiled Species

The legendary phoenix, ascending from its own remains, arises as a moral story for preservation endeavors. As jeopardized species face the phantom of elimination, the story of resurrection and restoration typified by the phoenix turns into a strong theme. Traditionalists draw motivation from these legendary accounts, entwining antiquated astuteness with contemporary provokes in the continuous battle to safeguard biodiversity.

4.3. Natural Pride and Useful examples

Folklore, through wake up calls like that of Icarus, cautions against ecological arrogance and the results of dismissing the cutoff points set commonly. The story of the goose that laid the brilliant eggs fills in as a piercing sign of the ecological results of uncontrolled ravenousness. These wake up calls reverberate with contemporary ecological difficulties, encouraging a reexamination of mankind's relationship with the regular world.

5. The Ease of Custom and Present day Transformations
5.1. Custom in Transition: Transformation and Reevaluation

The investigation has featured the unique idea of custom, where transformation and reevaluation revive antiquated accounts. From contemporary workmanship and writing to computerized stages and augmented realities, folklore tracks down articulation in different structures, resounding with developing sensibilities. The smoothness of custom fills in as a demonstration of its getting through pertinence and limit with respect to recharging.

5.2. Contemporary Stories: Folklore and Social Developments

In current settings, folklore crosses with social developments, giving stories that reverberate the yearnings and difficulties of contemporary society. From LGBTQ+ portrayal in fanciful transformations to the investigation of character legislative issues through avian gods, folklore turns into a no nonsense substance that draws in with the continuous discoursed within recent memory.

6. Folklore and the Human Journey for Significance
6.1. Greatness and the Heavenly Association

At the core of folklore lies the human journey for significance and association with the heavenly. Whether through creation fantasies, legend's excursions, or representative stories, folklore offers an otherworldly space where the natural and the heavenly unite. The investigation has enlightened the manners by which fantasies give roads to people to look for higher bits of insight and manufacture otherworldly associations.

6.2. Folklore as a Wellspring of Insight and Reflection

Folklore, with its immortal stories and model images, fills in as a wellspring of shrewdness and reflection. The getting through allure of these stories lies in their capacity to direct people through life's intricacies, offering experiences into human instinct, ethical quality, and the secrets of presence. The investigation has built up the possibility that folklore stays a wellspring of lasting pertinence, welcoming persistent consideration and understanding.

7. Looking Forward: Graphing Courses in Mythic Oceans
7.1. The Consistently Unfurling Mythic Odyssey
As we finish up this extensive investigation, it becomes obvious that the odyssey of folklore is consistently unfurling. Similarly as antiquated sailors explored strange oceans, we, as well, diagram courses into mythic domains that keep on motivating, challenge, and shape the accounts of our lives. The investigation has been a demonstration of the getting through force of fantasy to enlighten the human experience and guide us through the neglected regions of our aggregate creative mind.

7.2. Gatekeepers of Custom: Sustaining Legendary Legacy
In the stewardship of custom, we become gatekeepers of the mythic legacy went down through ages. The obligation to sustain these stories, adjust them to contemporary settings, and save their pith for people in the future is a holy trust. In doing as such, we add to the continuous discourse between the antiquated and the advanced, guaranteeing that the fire of folklore keeps on enlightening the human excursion.

8. Epilog: The Mythic Reverberations
8.1. The Reverberations Resonating Across Reality
As the investigation finishes up, the reverberations of mythic stories resonate across the huge breadth of human culture. From the booming conflict of divine beings on Mount Olympus to the sensitive shudder of a hummingbird's wings, each mythic reverberation resounds through the shared perspective. It welcomes us to tune in, to learn, and to convey forward the accounts that have molded civilizations and enlightened the way of humankind through the ages.

8.2. A Call to Proceed with the Investigation
This investigation is definitely not a last objective yet a call to proceed with the excursion into the mythic domains. The accounts are alive, ready to be rediscovered, reevaluated, and woven into the texture of our advancing stories. The mythic odyssey welcomes all who set out upon it to explore the oceans of creative mind, embracing the immortal insight found in the narratives that have reverberated through the passageways of time.

In the terrific finale of this odyssey through folklore, let the mythic reverberations wait, resounding in the shared awareness of humankind. May the investigation rouse new stories, ignite the fire of imagination, and cultivate an extended appreciation for the significant embroidery of legend that ties us to the timeless dance of divine beings, humans, and the universe. The odyssey proceeds, and the mythic reverberations persevere, coaxing all who set out to leave on the immortal journey through the domains of creative mind and significance.

8.1 Recap of key themes and findings

In our broad investigation of folklore, we've wandered across assorted social scenes, crossed the domains of divine beings and humans, and dove into the emblematic wealth of old accounts. As we set out on a recap of key topics and discoveries, the embroidery woven by these mythic strings uncovers significant bits of knowledge into the human experience, the transaction of imagery, and the getting through pertinence of legend across time and culture.

1. General Paradigms: Strings of Shared characteristic

At the core of folklore lies the acknowledgment of general paradigms that rise above social limits. Whether in the legend's excursion, the grandiose creation account, or the imagery of creatures, these paradigms go about as strings of shared characteristic that wind through the different texture of human narrating. The legend's mission for self-disclosure and the cyclic examples of creation and obliteration arise as immortal themes that reverberation across societies, interfacing mankind through shared stories.

2. Social Variety: Observing Mythic Hoards

While all inclusive originals structure a fundamental part of folklore, our investigation has featured the lavishness of social variety inside mythic customs. From the pantheons of Greek and Norse divine beings to the many-sided cosmologies of Hindu and Native folklores, each social woven artwork unfurls special stories that mirror the particular perspectives and upsides of their separate social orders. This variety commends the wealth of human creative mind as well as highlights the versatile idea of folklore to various social settings.

3. Folklore as a Reflection of Humankind

The narratives of divine beings and humans inside folklore act as mirrors mirroring the intricacies of the human experience. Whether investigating the ideals and indecencies epitomized by divinities or digging into the ethical issues looked by mortal legends, folklore offers significant experiences into the human condition. These stories give a system to figuring out the complexities of profound quality, mortality, and the enduring journey for implying that characterizes human life.

4. Representative Language of Folklore: Semiotics of the Heavenly

Folklore conveys through an emblematic language that rises above the restrictions of standard talk. Images, whether addressed by creatures, components, or inestimable themes, convey layers of implying that stretch out past the strict. Our investigation has disclosed the semiotics of the heavenly, uncovering how images go about as vessels for conveying significant insights, interfacing the natural with the extraordinary and encouraging a more profound comprehension of the secrets of presence.

5. Ecological Points of view in Folklore

An extraordinary part of our investigation has been the focal point through which we inspected folklore's natural viewpoints. Birds, as couriers, images, and natural markers, arose as captivating conductors for conveying ecological insight inside fanciful practices. Whether investigating the gatekeeper job of falcons or drawing matches between legendary phoenixes and protection moral stories, the fantasies delineated the antiquated acknowledgment of humankind's interconnectedness with the normal world.

6. Smoothness of Custom: Custom in Transition

The smoothness of custom has been a repetitive subject, underlining the flexibility of legend to changing social scenes. From antiquated oral practices to contemporary craftsmanship, writing, and computerized stages, folklore substantiates itself strong, ceaselessly developing to address the issues and sensibilities of every age. This flexibility fills in as a demonstration of the persevering through pertinence of fantasy as a powerful power in molding social personalities and stories.

7. Folklore and the Human Journey for Importance

Fundamental to the investigation has been the acknowledgment of folklore as a vessel for the human mission for importance. Through creation legends, legend's excursions, and representative stories, folklore offers an otherworldly space where people can look for higher bits of insight and fashion profound associations. The getting through allure of these stories lies in their capacity to direct people through life's intricacies, offering experiences into human instinct, ethical quality, and the secrets of presence.

8. The Crossing point of Folklore and Contemporary Settings

In the always developing social scene, folklore crosses with contemporary settings, adding to continuous discoursed and social developments. The investigation has disclosed occasions of folklore drawing in with LGBTQ+ portrayal, character legislative issues, and natural preservation in manners that reverberate with the goals and difficulties of contemporary society. This crossing point features the living, powerful nature of folklore as it keeps on developing close by the social outlook.

9. Folklore as a Wellspring of Shrewdness and Reflection

Folklore arises as an immortal wellspring of shrewdness and reflection, welcoming people to examine the intricacies of presence. The persevering through force of fantasies lies in their capacity to direct people through life's difficulties, offering bits of knowledge into human instinct, moral predicaments, and the everlasting dance among request and turmoil. As a wellspring of perpetual pertinence, folklore remains as a guide, enlightening the way of human comprehension and giving a structure to exploring the complexities of the human mind.

10. The Mythic Odyssey: Graphing Courses in Mythic Oceans
As we finish up our recap, we end up at the incline of the mythic odyssey. The investigation has been a demonstration of the steadily unfurling nature of legend, welcoming all who set out upon it to explore unknown oceans of creative mind and importance. In the stewardship of custom, we become gatekeepers of the mythic legacy, adding to the continuous exchange between the antiquated and the cutting edge.

11. Epilog: Reverberations Resonating Across Existence
In the last reverberates of our investigation, the resonating stories of divine beings, humans, and enormous powers wait across reality. The mythic reverberations persevere, coaxing all who set out to leave on the immortal journey through the domains of creative mind and significance. The investigation welcomes progressing consideration, understanding, and rediscovery, guaranteeing that the accounts of folklore keep on moving, challenge, and shape the stories of our aggregate human excursion.

8.2   The enduring significance of avian deities in contemporary society

In the tremendous embroidered artwork of human culture, the imagery and mythos encompassing avian gods have risen above the limits of old accounts, reverberating through the halls of time to track down reverberation in contemporary society. Birds, worshipped as couriers, images of amazing quality, and transporters of significant importance, keep on catching the aggregate creative mind. This investigation dives into the getting through meaning of avian divinities in current times, looking at how these old images have woven themselves into the texture of contemporary awareness, impacting workmanship, otherworldliness, and the human association with the normal world.

1. The Representative Flight: Birds as Couriers and Go-betweens
One of the persevering through parts of avian divinities lies in their job as couriers, filling in as go-betweens between the natural and the heavenly. In contemporary society, this imagery perseveres in different structures, reverberating through writing, workmanship, and, surprisingly, mainstream society.

1.1. Artistic Couriers: Owls and Ravens
The owl, frequently connected with shrewdness in Greek folklore, keeps on being a scholarly courier in contemporary works. J.K. Rowling's "Harry Potter" series, with the personality of Hedwig, epitomizes this congruity. The owl turns into an image of correspondence, conveying letters and messages between characters, spanning holes and fashioning associations.

Essentially, ravens, with their verifiable relationship with Odin in Norse folklore, wind up in present day accounts. George R.R. Martin's "A Melody of Ice and Fire" series, adjusted into the TV peculiarity "Round of High positions," highlights ravens as transporters of significant messages, connecting far off domains and assuming vital parts in the unfurling of the story.

1.2. Divine Messages: Innovation and Avian Imagery

During a time overwhelmed by innovation, the imagery of avian couriers has consistently converged with current correspondence. Email benefits frequently use bird images in their logos, summoning the possibility of quick, effective, and broad correspondence. The juxtaposition of old imagery with state of the art innovation features the ageless allure of avian gods as channels of messages.

2. Avian Gods in Contemporary Otherworldliness

As otherworldliness takes on different structures in contemporary society, avian gods keep on assuming a huge part as images of greatness, opportunity, and heavenly association.

2.1. Holy messengers with Wings: Christian Iconography

In Christianity, heavenly messengers with wings have become symbolic of guardian angels. The symbolism of holy messengers, frequently portrayed with wings looking like those of birds, highlights the relationship between the heavenly and the avian. This imagery endures in strict craftsmanship, supporting the possibility of holy messengers as go-betweens among paradise and earth.

2.2. Bird Emblems: Shamanic and New Age Practices

Shamanic and New Age profound practices frequently consolidate bird emblems as images of direction and higher information. Symbol creatures, including birds like falcons, birds of prey, and owls, are accepted to give profound bits of knowledge and act as defenders. People might look for association with these emblems for direction on their profound excursions, accentuating the persevering through faith in the otherworldly meaning of avian imagery.

3. Avian Gods in Craftsmanship and Mainstream society

The impact of avian gods expands conspicuously into the domains of craftsmanship and mainstream society, where their imagery is woven into the texture of narrating, visual expressions, and even design.

3.1. Design and Imagery: The Phoenix Rises

The legendary phoenix, representing resurrection and restoration, tracks down its place in contemporary style.

The picture of a rising phoenix, with its lively plumage, is a famous theme in dress plans and embellishments. This not just grandstands the stylish allure of avian imagery yet in addition underlines the getting through interest with topics of change and versatility.

3.2. Notable Logos: Owls and Corporate Character
Corporate logos frequently influence the imagery of birds to pass on messages of astuteness, trust, and unwavering quality. The owl, related with knowledge and wisdom, highlights in logos of instructive establishments, book shops, and monetary associations. This joining of avian images into corporate character highlights the getting through impression of birds as transporters of positive credits in contemporary society.

4. Protection and Ecological Mindfulness
In a period set apart by developing natural cognizance, avian gods take on new importance as images of preservation and biological equilibrium.

4.1. The Bald Eagle: Image of Protection Achievement
The bald eagle, a loved image of the US, offers a striking illustration of how avian gods become central focuses for protection endeavors. Once imperiled because of natural surroundings annihilation and pesticide use, coordinated preservation programs prompted the recuperation of the bald eagle populace. Today, the bald eagle stands as a public symbol as well as a demonstration of the effect of protection drives.

4.2. Ecological Missions: Involving Avian Imagery for Promotion
Birds, whether jeopardized or significant of explicit biological systems, are much of the time utilized in natural missions. Embellishing banners, logos, and online entertainment illustrations, avian images become mobilizing focuses for bringing issues to light about issues, for example, environment misfortune, environmental change, and the significance of biodiversity. The condor in South American legends, for example, becomes a social symbol as well as a point of convergence for protection endeavors pointed toward saving both the bird and its territory.

5. Avian Divinities and Social Developments
As cultural perspectives advance, avian divinities cross with contemporary social developments, impacting stories around personality, portrayal, and activism.

5.1. LGBTQ+ Portrayal: The Rainbow Association
Integrating avian divinities into LGBTQ+ portrayal is a strong illustration of how old imagery converges with contemporary social developments. The rainbow, related with LGBTQ+ pride, finds reverberations in the plumage of different birds.

This association serves not just as an image of variety and incorporation yet in addition as an extension between old fanciful stories and present day battles for acknowledgment and freedoms.

5.2. Character Governmental issues: The Thunderbird and Native Portrayal
In North American Native societies, the Thunderbird holds social importance as a strong and extraordinary figure. The Thunderbird turns into an image of flexibility and personality, impacting contemporary Native activism. The crossing point of avian imagery with personality legislative issues highlights the getting through force of old accounts in molding the talk around social portrayal and self-assurance.

6. Innovative Advances and Avian Mechanical technology
In a captivating union of old imagery and state of the art innovation, avian gods track down articulation in the field of mechanical technology.

6.1. Biomimicry: Automated Birds and Ethereal Advancement
Biomimicry, drawing motivation from nature for mechanical advancement, has prompted the improvement of automated birds. These counterfeit avians, with wings that imitate the mind boggling flight examples of genuine birds, grandstand the getting through impact of avian imagery on human creativity. The crossing point of folklore and innovation becomes evident as these mechanical manifestations give proper respect to the effortlessness and effectiveness of avian flight.

6.2. Drones and Winged Symbols: Present day Flying Symbolism
The utilization of robots for flying photography and reconnaissance brings avian imagery into contemporary applications. Drones, with their bird-like nimbleness and viewpoint, overcome any barrier between antiquated relationship of birds with higher vision and the mechanical progressions of the present. This mix of avian imagery into the domain of elevated innovation features the getting through engraving of birds on human ideas of flight and perception.

7. Avian Divinities in Virtual Domains: Gaming and Computerized Stories
As virtual domains become indispensable to present day amusement and narrating, avian gods end up adjusting to new mediums.

7.1. Gaming Symbols: The Bird of prey and the Computerized Skyline
In the gaming scene, avian divinities are in many cases embraced as strong symbols. The imagery of birds, like hawks, lines up with subjects of speed, accuracy, and elevated discernment, settling on them well known decisions for characters in computerized scenes.

The consistent mix of avian imagery into virtual domains delineates how antiquated stories continue and adjust inside the advancing spaces of diversion.

7.2. Computerized Narrating: Folklore in Virtual Universes
Computerized narrating stages and augmented reality encounters frequently integrate avian gods as focal components. These stories give clients vivid excursions that draw on old imagery, offering a contemporary method for drawing in with legendary topics. The converging of avian divinities with virtual narrating embodies the persevering through capacity of these images to dazzle and move across various mediums.

8. End: Wings of Emblematic Progression
The persevering through meaning of avian divinities in contemporary society is a demonstration of the immortal force of imagery, story, and the human association with the normal world. From writing to otherworldliness, from preservation to mechanical development, avian images continue as transporters of significance, adjusting to the advancing scenes of culture and awareness. As society keeps on winding around new stories, the wings of avian gods stay spread across the broad sky of human creative mind, interfacing the old with the cutting edge in a never-ending dance of representative progression.

8.3   Final thoughts on the universal appeal of birds in mythology
In the immense spread of human narrating, barely any themes have taken off as all around and enduringly as the emblematic presence of birds in folklore. From the lofty hawks of antiquated Greece to the mysterious phoenix of Egyptian legend, birds have woven themselves into the texture of social stories across the globe. As we consider the general allure of birds in folklore, it becomes clear that these winged animals rise above geological limits, social contrasts, and fleeting distances, making a permanent imprint on the aggregate human creative mind.

1. A Culturally diverse Ensemble: Birds as Mythic Originals
The widespread allure of birds in folklore is established in their model imagery that rises above social lines. The theme of birds as couriers, images of opportunity, and delegates between the natural and the heavenly reverberations across different mythic customs. Whether it's the raven of Norse folklore, the peacock in Hindu legend, or the quetzal in Mesoamerican societies, the prototype reverberation of birds associates mankind through a common emblematic language.

1.1. Couriers of the Heavenly
Birds, with their capacity to cross the domains of the sky, have been all around saw as couriers of the heavenly. This imagery is reflected in legends where divine beings and

goddesses utilize birds to pass their will on to humans. The pigeon, for example, is a steady courier in different social stories, representing harmony, trust, and heavenly blessing.

1.2. Images of Opportunity and Greatness
The symbolism of birds in flight, taking off across the sky, represents opportunity and greatness. This subject is obvious in the Greek legend of Daedalus and Icarus, where the wax-winged flight turns into an illustration for the human quest for opportunity, desire, and the longing to rise above natural limits. Comparative themes show up in societies around the world, underscoring the widespread human yearning for freedom.

1.3. Mediators Between Universes
Birds frequently act as mediators between the natural and otherworldly domains. In Hindu folklore, Garuda goes about as the mount of Vishnu, spanning the earthly and divine areas. The Thunderbird in Native societies and the heavenly creatures with wings in Christian practices comparably typify this job, mirroring a common human requirement for channels that interface the everyday with the otherworldly.

2. Birds as Reflectors of Human Experience
The getting through allure of birds in folklore lies in their capacity to reflect and enhance features of the human experience. Whether through the resonant songbird of Greek fantasies or the craftiness crow in different old stories, birds act as mirrors that catch the ideals, imperfections, and intricacies of mankind.

2.1. Imagery of Ethics and Indecencies
Birds are frequently permeated with emblematic characteristics that reflect ethics or indecencies. The relationship of the owl with intelligence or the peacock with vanity represents how these avian images act as figurative mirrors for human credits. Such imagery welcomes thought on temperances to be worshipped and imperfections to be survived, encouraging moral contemplation.

2.2. Original Characters in Human Show
Birds much of the time assume jobs as model personalities in the terrific show of human life. The phoenix, with its repeating demise and resurrection, turns into a strong image of versatility, trust, and the timeless pattern of life. These avian prime examples become ageless aides, offering accounts that resound with the human mission for importance, reason, and existential comprehension.

3. Birds as Natural Gatekeepers and Signs

The widespread allure of birds in folklore stretches out to their jobs as natural gatekeepers and signs. Across societies, birds are frequently viewed as harbingers of progress, marks of regular peculiarities, and gatekeepers of the environments they possess.

3.1. Watchmen of Nature

In Native societies, certain birds like the falcon or the condor are adored as gatekeepers of nature. Their presence and conduct are viewed as signs of the strength of biological systems, underlining the interconnectedness among birds and the climate. This point of view keeps on impacting contemporary ecological perspectives, featuring the persevering through pertinence of birds as natural images.

3.2. Signs and Prognostications

Birds, through their flight examples, calls, or appearances, are frequently deciphered as signs or prognostications. The crow's cawing, for instance, has been generally connected with different understandings across societies, from proclaiming demise to meaning a message from the soul world. These understandings mirror a common human tendency to look for significance and direction from the normal world, particularly from animals with a magical emanation like birds.

4. The Ageless Dance: Birds in the Enormous Artful dance

Birds in folklore frequently partake in the vast artful dance, encapsulating divine powers, and adding to the creation and request of the universe. The divine dance of birds addresses the general human interest with the universe and the interconnectedness of every living being.

4.1. Vast Creation and Request

In numerous creation fantasies, birds assume a vital part in the foundation of grandiose request. The Chinese fantasy of the goddess Nüwa, who repairs the sky with the assistance of astronomical birds, epitomizes this topic. Birds, in this specific circumstance, become specialists of vast agreement, underscoring the interconnectedness of the divine and natural domains.

4.2. Heavenly Route and Groups of stars

Birds, both genuine and legendary, are frequently connected with divine route and the arrangement of groups of stars. The swan in Greek folklore, the divine goose in Native legend, and the magnificent peacock in Hindu cosmology all add to the enormous dance of stars and act as tokens of the multifaceted connection between natural stories and the boundlessness of the universe.

5. The Development of Imagery: Birds in Contemporary Points of view

As society develops, so too does the imagery encompassing birds. In contemporary points of view, birds keep on charming the human creative mind, impacting craftsmanship, writing, and, surprisingly, forming ecological and protection endeavors.

5.1. Birds in Workmanship and Writing

The getting through allure of birds is substantial in the domain of craftsmanship and writing. From canvases and figures to sonnets and books, birds act as dreams for imaginative articulation. Specialists and scholars draw on the imagery, folklore, and stylish charm of birds to pass on messages of magnificence, opportunity, and profound amazing quality in their works.

5.2. Birds as Ecological Symbols

During a time of expanded ecological mindfulness, birds have become symbols for preservation and biodiversity. Jeopardized species like the California condor or the Kakapo in New Zealand, with their tricky presence, evoke endeavors for their protection. The gooney bird, with its imagery of route and perseverance, turns into a point of convergence for crusades tending to plastic contamination in the seas. These contemporary stories highlight the advancing meaning of birds as images of ecological obligation.

6. End: Wings Across Time and Culture

All in all, the general allure of birds in folklore is a demonstration of the getting through force of imagery and narrating in molding the human experience. Birds rise above transient and social limits, winding around an embroidery of significance, reflection, and goal. Whether filling in as couriers of the heavenly, reflectors of human temperances and indecencies, or gatekeepers of the climate, birds keep on resounding across the ages, welcoming mankind to go along with them in the immortal dance of legend and imagery. As we focus on the skies, the wings of these legendary animals spread across time and culture, welcoming us to take off with them into the limitless domains of creative mind and understanding.